NOT SO DUSTY
TALES OF AN ANTIQUARIAN BOOKDEALER

By Anthony Chandor

First printing, 2013

ISBN-13: 978-1494211981
ISBN-10: 149421198X

Cover and interior illustrations copyright © 2013 by Timothy Jaques
Book design by Matt Kaiser

iPad® is a registered trademark of Apple Inc., registered in the U.S. and other countries
Kindle® is a registered trademark of Amazon.com, registered in the U.S. and other countries

ACKNOWLEDGEMENTS

With grateful thanks, I acknowledge the help of:

Noel Rae, of New York, who more or less forced me to write this

Sandy Barton, of Buffalo, for her calm and continued support

George Kimball, of Bath, whose sensitive editing was so valuable

Evelyn Heavens, of Bitton, who led the whole Heavens family
in enthusiastic and helpful encouragement

Joshua Billig, who was so helpful at the early stages

For my darling Maryanne
who died on November 1st, 2012

CONTENTS

THE BEGINNING 1

I: THE AUCTION 7

II: THE WEDNESDAY MARKET 17

III: THE BOOKSHOP 35

IV: DRAMATIS PERSONAE 49

V: THIEVES 81

VI: FAIRS AND RINGS 93

VII: HOUSE CALLS 111

VIII: THE COLLECTOR 129

IX: DEALING 147

X: THE GOOD, THE BAD, AND THE BED-BOUND 169

VOCABULARY 187

NOT SO DUSTY

THE BEGINNING

I did not set out in life to become an antiquarian bookdealer. But then, neither did anyone else I have met since joining this curious fraternity some 20 years ago. It is not, after all, a profession one can prepare for at a university. Nor is it the sort of vocation one might have dreamt of as a child-like becoming a famous explorer, or a handsome film star, or someone fiendishly clever in the City, (all of which I seriously considered at one time or another in my youth). In my experience, antiquarian bookdealers have either grudgingly taken a place in a family firm after having done badly at something else, or have entered the business in early or later middle life seeking new stimulus, or new horizons, or because they believed it was easier and more profitable than doing what they were then doing, or as in my case, due to unforeseen circumstances . . .

My circumstances arrived one sunny spring morning in 1984, when Simon Lacey, senior partner in our accountants, Hawkes Mayhew, walked into my West End office and announced without preamble: "You'll have to go into voluntary liquidation, Anthony. This man Samson has done you over for £120,000. All of your working capital is gone. So is he. The police assure me they'll do what they can to find him - but don't hold your breath."

"What on earth do you mean?"

"I mean what I say. You're out of business, and the sooner you recognise it the better. I'll do what I can to help, but the quicker we act the better."

So Samson was indeed the Scampson I had always secretly called him. He was a really good project manager, and I had had no cause to complain, but there was something arrogant about his manner that was distasteful. Rot his guts. I think he would not have thought himself in the least dishonest to write out cheques for £80,000 and £40,000 (not large enough to ring any alarm bells in our bank manager's ears) and leave for a comfortable six months on the Costa del Crime. He would think himself pretty clever and would sleek back his ginger hair in quiet self-adoration.

The two contracts he was managing for us were Government ones, each nearing completion without being replaced by more work - something of a crime in itself: all consultants know that any consultancy contract should end only with the death of one party.

I did some quick mental arithmetic and established that we had about enough money to pay outstanding VAT and corporate tax bills, rent and rates, the payroll for the next month and probably something I had forgotten so long as it wasn't too monstrous. The staff wouldn't find it difficult to secure new jobs, though they might not get jobs as well paid and might have to gulp for a month or two before getting used to slightly lower pay cheques. Even if it wasn't so bad for them, I felt really guilty, especially for the three senior ones who had all worked for me before and for whom I felt the loyalty any manager feels for staff he has recruited himself.

My business, built up from scratch, consisted of hiring out skilled programmers to help customers working on large projects and unwilling to hire their own staff. It was called 'body-shopping' in the trade, and was considered a little disreputable. Even so, we also won a number of contracts to do all the work from initial detailed definition of the project down to delivery of working, tested software. At the moment we employed eighty programmers, thirty of whom were working on self-contained projects, while the others were all working for regular customers, earning good fees for us. The company was my baby and I was proud of it, proud of the high quality of the staff, proud of our reputation for delivering good work, and proud of the fact that nearly a hundred people lived comfortable lives as our employees.

My mind raced. How had it happened? I should have to write to all of them - the same letter explaining the situation and assuring them of a good reference, perhaps with a personal note to each. Next I would have to write to each customer giving notice that our staff would be withdrawn in a month, and giving them freedom to enter into a new arrangement with the staff they were hiring from us. Then I should talk to the secretarial staff, the telephonists, cleaners, all the people I had trained so carefully and who had been so important to the company. And our landlords. And a hundred other things.

Most importantly - how was I to tell Maryanne? She would take it on the chin of course, as she had done over other disasters in our lives, and between us we would think of some way of rising from these ashes. We would have to tell the children, too. No more sleek company car. No more money at all. I smiled a little: no more money for Hawkes Mayhew. I turned to listen to Simon Lacey as he sketched out the process of voluntary liquidation. Some hours later, I caught the last train home to Haslemere.

My flourishing thirty-year career in computing was over. I was jobless, futureless, colleague-less and thanks to all the good times I'd had at Oxford, not properly prepared to do anything else to earn a living. Everyone always said that it was impossible to find a job when you were past fifty and I realised that this was probably true. I thought of the conversations which had taken place over the past ten years in which the possibility of my changing jobs was discreetly hinted at. None of them would look at me now, with a track record ending in liquidation. And I didn't think I had the energy to start another software house, even if I wasn't haunted by the label 'Failure'. No, it would have to be something completely outside the computer indus-try. I had written several books about computers and these had each generated some pleasing revenue, but I couldn't think of anything fresh to write about. No, any way of earning a living would have to be something completely new, and probably outside London.

Was I too old to start a career in teaching? I probably wouldn't be much good at it. And the same certainly applied to anything attractive, like professional golfer or sports commentator. I was too old and unqualified. The days of the commercial traveller were long gone, and anyway my feet weren't really up to walking from door-to-door while I carried a suitcase growing heavier with each step.

What I did have were a wife whom I loved inordinately, two

thoroughly admirable children, and a large house in Surrey. Obviously, decisions had to be made. By the end of summer, Maryanne and I had made them: we would sell the big house in Haslemere, use the bulk of the money to clear our professional and personal debts, and spend whatever was left over making a new life for ourselves somewhere else. I had just turned 54. The somewhere else we chose was Bath, and our new life, we decided, would be sustained by the only thing Maryanne and I knew and cared enough about to let us hope we might make a go of it . . .

******

"Books," I announced to the children the following week-end.

"Books," our son, Nicholas, said.

"Rare and antiquarian ones," said Maryanne, "plus modern first editions."

"Buying and selling," I added, "not writing."

"Do you know anything about doing that?" our daughter asked. Sarah is the practical one in the family.

"I'm confident he'll learn," Maryanne answered.

We were gathered in the dining room of our newly purchased garden flat in Brock Street, the street that connects the King's Circus to the Royal Crescent; renowned for its handsome Georgian terraces and the frequency of its tourist buses. I sat at the foot of the eighteenth century oval dining table we'd rescued from the house sale two months previously. Nicholas, aged 23, who owned a trendy antiques shop in Notting Hill, sat to my left and Sarah, 24, who had recently moved to Bath with her young son Charles following her divorce the year before, sat to my right with a note pad in front of her. Maryanne, wearing her best no-nonsense expression, sat facing us from the head of the table and when she said, "I'm confident he'll learn," we all knew she meant it - and we all knew I would.

"In my view," Nicholas offered, with great seriousness, "you have four special assets for the antiquarian book trade: you are large, you are bald, you are jovial and you look like a character in a Dickens novel."

Right on all counts, but the fact that my son (and indeed my daughter) are both cleverer than I, does not, as any father will agree, give them the right to prove it in front of their mother, (who is, of course, also cleverer than I).

"Is that what you call a useful contribution?" I asked, (devastating wit).

"Of course," said Nicholas, quite unruffled.

"He's talking about trust, Dad," said Sarah. "You look trust-worthy."

"And you look as if you know stuff about books," said Nicholas.

"And people like you," said Sarah.

"You remind them of their teddy bears when they were little," said Nicholas.

"That's an enormous asset," said Sarah.

"Huge!"

I looked down the table at Maryanne. She tilted her head side-ways. All true then. I had special assets. In abundance! This was going to work, by God!

We took a break for tea in our new garden - Earl Grey with Mary-anne's home-made scones and Sarah's home-made blueberry jam. The autumn sun shone down. Birds larked about in the honeysuck-le. A grumpy-looking frog who would in time become a loyal friend watched us from the shell of an ornamental stone pelican in the bub-bling pond by the terrace. We finished the jam, cleared the tea things, scattered scone crumbs for the birds, then returned to the table to map out a strategy for me to become a successful antiquarian book-dealer in as short a time as possible. (I only learned it some months later, but the title "antiquarian bookdealer" is pure sham. What we all buy and sell are second hand books. But "second hand" sounds down-market, which we are not, so we style ourselves "Antiquarian" or "Rare" for reasons of simple self-regard. In insider jargon, "anti-quarian" actually means any book a hundred or more years old that has lost its dust wrapper; while "rare" is any book which, "We haven't a copy in stock just now, Madam." A dust wrapper, incidentally, is the proper name for what other people call a dust jacket. Why anyone cares about this distinction has always been beyond me. I adhere to it, however, because my fellow traders might think me a trouble-maker if

I didn't. I will, on occasion, even correct the uninitiated on the subject; with great kindness, of course, carefully concealing any hint of smugness I might be enjoying.)

It was agreed all round that the sooner I got started in my new life the better for everyone - and for our bank balance. It was also agreed that I should begin at the beginning by learning the tricks and pitfalls of the book auction (one of the four basic ways a bookdealer acquires stock, the others being house calls, offers made in shop, and purchases on the Internet – all discussed in later chapters). To do that with a minimum of blunders, I knew I would need a mentor, but I didn't know any mentors. Maryanne did.

"He's called Peter Goodden," she said. "Highly respected."

"He's a friend of Charles," said Sarah. Charles being Sarah's first husband, who, following a run of rather dashing vicissitudes, had himself, ended up an independent bookdealer in London. High End stuff, though; nothing under five figures.

"I saw Peter yesterday," Maryanne went on. "There's a Victorian auction on Tuesday afternoon at Bath Brown's." She skated a catalogue down the table to me. "He said to give you this, so you can do your homework." Clipped to the cover was Peter's telephone number. "You can ring him on Monday evening and arrange to meet there. He said he'd be happy to show you the ropes."

"You're all set then," Nicholas said. "By teatime on Tuesday you'll be a bookdealer."

"Just like that?"

"Just like that."

"But don't I need a shop?"

"Ropes first," Maryanne said.

CHAPTER ONE: THE AUCTION

"We met without difficulty."

Auctions were by no means a mystery to me. I'd been attending them since Oxford days - first alone, later with Maryanne - bidding for pictures, bits of china, books, the occasional piece of furniture - but always as a private buyer, never as a "professional" acquiring stock to resell. And as Peter soon made clear, there was a critical difference.

I spent most of Monday afternoon in the garden making ticks in my catalogue beside books I might want to bid for, then rang Peter after supper and arranged to meet outside Bath Brown's at ten the next morning.

"Have you marked up your catalogue?" he asked.

"Diligently," I said.

"Good man. Do you know the bookdealers' code?"

"The what?"

"Never mind, I'll explain when I see you. Do you know how to get to the auction house?"

"Brock Street to the Circus," I said. "Then down Gay Street to the top of Queen's Square, then left into that little street whose name no one remembers and it's on my right fifty yards along."

"That's it," said Peter. "A big, square pile, like a prison. Does its best to look Georgian, but it was actually built after the war on a bomb site. Deserves sympathy for that, I suppose. Pretty gloomy to spend time in, though. How shall I know you, Anthony?"

I said I was large, bald and looked something like a teddy bear.

"I am bald and large, too," Peter said. "Fat, actually. And quite disagreeable-looking."

We met without difficulty.

As today's auction was scheduled for 2 p.m. and viewing didn't begin until eleven, Peter suggested a second breakfast at a cafe around the corner where he could do some introductory mentoring.

"Excellent," I said, "as long as you don't tell my wife about the second breakfast." And off we went.

"As far as bookdealers are concerned," Peter began, when we'd taken seats at a corner table and been given our coffees and croissants, "auctions are for one thing only: acquiring stock which can be resold at a profit."

I nodded.

"No serious bookdealer will go anywhere near a book auction except for that reason - and that reason alone!" The last three words accompanied by three stabs of the table with his index finger.

My first solemn lesson, apparently. Meaning what, I couldn't imagine. It sounded more like a confession of personal weakness than mentoring. But it was clearly not to be taken lightly, so I simply nodded again and tried to look chastened.

"A book auction," Peter then went on, "is like any other auction, except that it moves very, very quickly. A good auctioneer can get through 120 lots in an hour, so concentration is essential. If you spot a pretty girl across the sale room and daydream for only half-a-minute before remembering you are 50-something and look like a stuffed toy, you will surely discover that the one lot you wanted desperately to compete for has already been called and sold.

So, be forewarned - concentration is everything!" and he gave the table-top another poke.

"A lot," he then continued, "may comprise a single book or several. If you want only one book in a multiple lot, you still have to buy the whole batch. You bid on a lot by raising your hand, or your catalogue, or anything else you choose to wave in the air so that the auctioneer can identify you instantly, and knows you are still in the bidding. You drop out by not raising whatever it is. If the auctioneer looks at you, you may shake your head 'no' - polite, but not obligatory. If you make a successful bid, you must hold up the numbered paddle you'll be given when you register so the auctioneer can mark your paddle number against the lot number in his list. That's all there is to it. At the end, you go to Accounts and pay for any lots you've bid on successfully. Accounts add on the auctioneer's percentage, give you a receipt, and you take that to Collections where they give you your books."

"Like buying a toaster at Argos," I said.

"Very like," said Peter. "But that's the easy part."

"And the hard part . . .?"

"The viewing," he said. "Ascertaining the condition of every lot you've marked for bidding, then settling on a top limit for each based on that, your profit margin requirements, your overall budget for the day, and the auctioneer's estimate of each book's value, which in turn will be based on prices the book has made in previous auctions."

"Sounds straightforward enough," I said.

Peter shook his head. "Anything but," he replied, "as any number of failed bookdealers will be happy to tell you. At length. Over drinks. Lots of them. That *you* pay for . . . "

He then explained the ritual of pre-auction registration; a procedure in which I would be obliged to identify myself at Accounts to roughly MI5 standards and then hand over my banking details for verification. Payment for lots won, he said, was always made by cheque or in cash, never by credit card. A fee had to be paid for credit card transactions, and auction houses didn't pay fees. Auction houses existed for the sole purpose of taking money. Not giving it away. Especially not for the convenience of insignificant bookdealers.

We paid our bill and strolled back toward Bath Brown's in the sunshine while Peter outlined the basics of collating a book one plans to bid for. The verb collate, he explained, actually meant the interleaving of one set of something - cards, for example - with another. When used by bookdealers, it meant the careful checking and noting of every physical detail of a book one has already purchased so that prospective buyers can be assured that the book is exactly as described, warts and all.

"When viewing books at auction, however," Peter went on, "dealers simply use the term collate as short-hand for checking if a book's condition corresponds to its description in the auctioneer's catalogue."

Doing that, he explained, requires going through it page by page to make sure all of its pages are there, that all of the plates in illustrated books are intact, and that any pages or the binding have not suffered damage by water, heat, children, pets, etc., that has not been noted in the catalogue. If the auctioneer has done his job properly, book and description will match, and the estimated value he has placed on it will be more or less fair. If he hasn't done a proper job - and there are endless reasons for that happening, Peter assured me - the naive and trusting newcomer (me) may find he has paid miles over the odds for a book he may never be able to resell, much less make a profit on. And all because he hasn't done his own job properly.

"Which is collating," I said.

"Correct," said Peter. "With great rigour."

I said I certainly would apply myself rigorously to my collating, as we climbed the three steps to Bath Brown's wide porch, entered a cavernous, dimly-lit foyer and crossed to a long counter marked ACCOUNTS where two middle-aged women of formidable bearing seemed to be trying to make anyone who approached them feel small. Peter led me to the nearest of these women, showed her his identification, introduced me as a new Bath bookdealer and asked politely, if I might register. She eyed me suspiciously for a long moment, then produced a form from beneath her counter and handed it to me with a ball-point pen: Name, business name, home address, trading address, contact telephones, email, banking particulars, criminal record, if any, (details on a separate sheet, please) . . .

When I got to the space marked "business name", I put "Bankes Books". I'd thought initially to use my own name, Chandor, but Maryanne, thought not. Her family name, she assured me, was more euphonious, easier to remember, sounded attractively alliterative and enjoyed a certain historical cachet. I agreed. "Besides," she'd said, "no-one will be able to pronounce your fine old Hungarian name."

"Fine old Hungarians might," I suggested hopefully . . .

So "Bankes Books" it would be. I signed my completed registration form, handed it back, waited while a telephone call to my bank confirmed that I was indeed good for what I'd claimed I was good for, and was then given a wooden paddle bearing the number 388. "I expect you know what to do with this," the formidable Lady Gatekeeper said. "If not, I'm sure Mr. Goodden will demonstrate." She gave us both an icy smile, and turned away to intimidate another poor dealer who'd just approached her counter.

"You'll have plenty of time for viewing," Peter said, leading me down the foyer toward Brown's sale room. "But I'm afraid you'll have to do that on your own. What happens next is the way I earn my living - and the way you'll be earning yours from now on - so I won't have time to stand about giving you advice. I won't be with you during bidding, either. I shall be at the back of the room with the old pros where the auctioneer expects to see us. I suggest you sit in the middle toward the front where the auctioneer can spot you easily. You'll find lots of comfy sofas and chairs to sit on - hundreds, actually - there's a general sale on later today. I also suggest you find a quiet corner out here now and go through your catalogue once more, making any last minute notes you think might help. Then go into the sale room and examine each lot you've chosen to bid for. And remember, be ruthless with yourself. Don't, for heaven's sake, ever think, 'Oh, this is a book I'd love to own, think only Ah ha! This is a book my customers will fight over like animals!'"

I assured Peter I would follow this advice to the letter, said I'd meet him back here after the sale, and settled myself in an ancient leather armchair near the coat racks to give my chosen prey a final review. It didn't take long. Only three books that fell within my

first-timer budget had actually earned ticks: a Surtees with plates by
Leech, an eighteenth century treatise on surgery, and a collection of
Byron's Works. All of these were single lots. I'd also marked half a
dozen further singles with question marks, meaning possibly to bid,
but only if the competition was at best tepid. Multiple lots, because
they might comprise 30 or more books of wildly varying value,
weren't described book by book in the catalogue. Instead, they were
entered as a "lead title", followed by the total number of books in the
lot and an estimated price for all. A typical example was lot 57: 40
books, estimated at £20 - £30, "led" by an 1890 copy of *The Strand*
magazine containing a first printing of a Sherlock Holmes story. This
sounded a brilliant find but in fact wasn't. The magazine, I knew,
would have been printed in the tens of thousands, and at least five
thousand Conan Doyle enthusiasts or their heirs who still possessed a
copy would have hung onto it believing it was the only one left in existence. I did mark one lead title for possible bidding though, a Kipling
Just So Stories in French (*Comme ci, comme ca*) that just might, intuition
whispered, have slipped the radar. Then . . .

Beginner beware! I said to myself, as I rose like Henry V armed
with my catalogue and paddle, strode confidently to the end of the
foyer, pushed open the double doors marked SALE, and, just as Peter
had promised, walked into a vast, echoing hall full of Victorian furniture.

"You'll find the lots are arranged in numerical order on tables
under the windows," he'd said, "with scores of scowling dealers paw-
ing over them like ferrets - and not a word being spoken. All you'll
hear is the sound of pages being turned and the occasional despairing
grunt."

The Surtees I'd marked, *Mr. Sponge's Sporting Tour*, was a first edition in very good condition, just as the catalogue promised. No missing pages, or tears, or foxing, or children's scribbles, or grown-ups'
marginal notes. John Leech's splendid illustrations were all intact, too.
(It was Leech, also known as 'Blicky', a life-long friend of Thackeray's, whose comic engraving in an 1843 edition of *Punch*, is believed
to have been the first satirical drawing ever referred to as a cartoon.)
I then moved on along the tables until I found the surgery book

I wanted to try for. Beginning to feel a proper professional already, I examined this with enthusiasm and great care. It was a handsome-looking quarto, with full calf binding and again, all its plates intact. One of these, which was noted in the catalogue as "slightly damaged", bore a well-aged spattering of what looked like a good Burgundy spilt across the bottom. Slight damage notwithstanding, I again marked the top estimate as the level I would bid to. I collated the Byron next, then went on to my question-marked singles, examined and priced each of them with no less rigour, and finally returned to the first table to start doing the multiples.

I began with the boxed lot "led" by *The Strand Sherlock Holmes*, which I certainly didn't want, but I scrambled through the rest of the box anyway, because the multiples, known in the trade as "The Field of Dreams", was where very occasionally a "sleeper" might be unearthed: a first edition of a forgotten early novel by an author who later became a giant; or, according to one of the legends of the auction rooms, an offspring of that scruffy-looking *Dr. No*, bought in a £10 multiple in Brighton, that subsequently made several thousand at Christies when the child's scribbled face on the inside back cover, turned out to be a portrait of Ian Fleming drawn by Sean Connery. Alas, I found no equivalent sleepers in *The Strand* box. I found no sleepers at all. However, I went diligently through the other multiples, quickly studying each book, calculating that if I had a bookshop and needed to stock its shelves I could safely bid £20 for any of these boxes and still come out ahead by pricing each book at £2 or £3. But I didn't have a bookshop yet, and if I had, I wouldn't have needed stock immediately. I already had a thousand or so books we'd brought from Haslemere in storage, plus a houseful of books bought from a friend of Maryanne's whose parents had recently died, plus all the books I'd inherited from my own parents. Nevertheless, I did my job as instructed - and just as I finished examining the last book in the last box of multiples, a clock struck two somewhere in the building, the auctioneer strode briskly to the rostrum, gave his gavel a resounding whack, and we began.

"How was it?" Maryanne asked, as I walked into the kitchen at five o'clock, with my shopping bags full of treasures . . .

"Exciting," I said. "I think I'm going to like this business."

"I want to hear everything."

We took glasses of wine, a bowl of cashews and my books into the garden.

"From the beginning, please," Maryanne said.

I told her about meeting Peter outside Bath Brown's and about all the cautionary tutoring he'd given me over coffee before viewing began (leaving out the croissants). I described registering with the gorgon, then going into the sale room and carefully examining the single lots I'd marked in my catalogue, assigning bidding limits to each, then going through all the multiple trays looking for surprises. I felt very professional, and totally in control, I assured her - until the bidding began. Then a fog of excitement and panic descended, and before I knew it lot 4 had been called and I'd bought ". . . A very handsomely bound *Works of Byron* in full red calf . . ." for a world record price of £50. Except that it was the wrong Byron. I'd wanted to bid for lot 40, not lot 4.

"This?" Maryanne said, taking it from the bag.

I nodded.

"Oh dear."

"I know."

"What did Peter say, afterwards?"

"That the binding was nice, but perhaps I wouldn't get back what I'd paid for it."

"Sounds right."

"At least there must have been an under bidder at £45," I offered, feebly. At which point I went into the kitchen to refill the cashew bowl. When I got back, Maryanne had the surgery book open in front of her.

"What's this red mark?" she said, looking up from the illustrations.

"Nuits-St-Georges, I think."

"Didn't you spot it during viewing?"

I said of course I had spotted it, but that I believed the book would make a good profit anyway, and had even invented a story explaining the stain's presence which might, if believed, enhance its value further.

"What story . . . ?"

"That the stain isn't wine at all, but blood spattered on the plate during an emergency field operation at Balaclava."

"You can't tell anyone that," Maryanne giggled, "it's unscrupulous."

"Funny - that's exactly what Peter said." I finished my wine and put my glass down:

"He also said I clearly had the makings of a first rate bookseller."

CHAPTER TWO: THE WEDNESDAY MARKET

"Her moustache was rather less conspicuous."

Flattering, perhaps, however ironic, but the truth was I had never sold a book for profit in my life, and before I could even contemplate owning a bookshop, I needed to prove to myself that I could actually make a living at it. I consulted Peter over the week-end, and early the following Monday, dressed in my most bookseller-ish suit and tie, I walked across the Circus to Bennett Street, skirted past the Assembly Rooms, continued down to the Bartlett Street Market, found my way to the manager's office and announced that I wished to become a stall-holder.

"When?" he asked, looking up from his desk. He was a meagre, mournful-looking man, with a jet black comb-over and drooping black moustache - both obviously dyed.

"As soon as possible," I said.

"What do you sell?"

"Books."

"Books," he said, opened a tatty brown ledger on his desk,

produced a magnifying glass, and began humming and hawing as he turned over pages. A minute went by, then two. I prepared myself to hear that there might be space for me in five or six months' time - if I was lucky.

"How about the day after tomorrow?" he said.

It took a moment to register, then, "Fine," I said. "Splendid."

"A space downstairs has just come available," he said. "Sam Crierly. Nice fella. Botanical Illustrations. Beautiful. Totally unexpected. My daughter will show you."

He called through a curtain behind him and a young woman appeared a moment later.

"This is Ellie," he said. "I'm Stanley, by the way."

Ellie was nearly identical to her father - except younger, of course, and her moustache was rather less conspicuous.

"Follow me," she said, and led me out of the office and down a wide sweep of stone steps into the market's basement sale rooms.

"There," she said, pointing.

In a corner under the stairs we'd just descended was a rectangular space enclosed by walls on two sides, that I estimated would accommodate enough shelving to display five or six hundred books with a little space left over for me. I glanced around the room in the half dark, trying to imagine how it would look two days hence with all the lights switched on and a roomful of dealers and buyers crowding eagerly from stall to stall, chattering and bargaining, drinking takeaway coffee and noisily doing deals.

"I think this will be fine," I said. "Excellent, in fact."

Bath is no longer the antiques centre it once was. But in the days when Maryanne and I first moved here, it was still renowned among dealers from all over Britain as a kind of West-country Samarkand. There were two big auction houses holding sales every Tuesday and Friday alternatively - Kimball's being one of them - and three markets, this one, the Guinea Lane Market and one I always thought of as "The Red Chaise" - because it had one in place of a sign on the porch roof over its entry. All were situated within a radius of two streets, and all of them operated on Wednesdays only, but staggered their opening hours so that out-of-town traders could comfortably visit all three in a single day. The Bartlett Street Market, also called the Stanley Market, opened earliest and was the largest of the three, comprising this basement room, which comfortably accommodated forty stalls, plus two more floors upstairs of similar size; the topmost of which also boasted a restaurant that served an amazingly good breakfast. Buyers and traders in everything from cloisonné to comic books would get up at three o'clock in the morning in London or Manchester in order to be here by six when the doors opened. And for local dealers, Peter told me, being a stall-holder here was like having a license to print money - if, that is, you had things people really wanted . . .

And could sell them, I thought to myself, taking a last edgy look at my new place of business.

"I feel very lucky," I said to Ellie, as we headed back up the stairs to her father's office. "But I am also very sorry about Mr. Crierly."

"Why?" she said.

"Because you couldn't have offered me his space if he were still with us."

"With us . . . ?" she frowned, then smiled suddenly: "Oh. No - Sam didn't die. He ran off with Eldon Rafferty's wife last week. Telephoned yesterday to say he'd be giving up the stall."

A kind of luck, I suppose - though maybe not for the unfortunate Mr. Rafferty.

I told Stanley I would take the space, and after shaking hands he proceeded to explain that the rent, £35, would be collected on Wednesday, a week in advance; that the stall must be manned at all times on Wednesdays; that while etiquette in the basement was less exacting than upstairs (he actually used the word "exacting"), decorum was still expected to be strictly maintained at all times: including cleanliness and tidiness of both stall and stall-holder, a reasonable degree of sobriety, no improper language beyond the usual, and generally polite behaviour toward customers and fellow stall-holders, alike. He then asked me where I lived, was I married, and would I be able to pay the rent on time. I answered Brock Street, yes and yes, which appeared to satisfy him. Finally he asked me how long I planned to keep the stall. I said six months to a year, ample time, I reckoned, to discover if I really could sell books.

"Right then," he said. "We'll be open tomorrow from 2 p.m. until four for setting up. You can safely leave everything here; the building is guarded and no one has access, even stall-holders, outside trading hours. You'll need folding bookshelves - nine I reckon, for that particular space - plus a dozen book boxes and a book table. I can do those for . . ." and he named an extortionate, three-figure sum. I thanked him but said I already had everything I needed for the stall, wrote a cheque for this and next Wednesday's rent, and said I would see him tomorrow at two o'clock.

"I can probably do a bit better on those shelves," he called after me as I went out of the door. I waved and kept going, pretending I hadn't heard him.

******

At ten minutes to two the next afternoon, I parked my old Volvo outside the market's big basement doors and began unloading: seven folding shelves (known as "thumb-pinchers" in the trade - acquired from one of those bankrupt dealers Peter had told me about earlier); 34 boxes of books; an old biscuit tin full of rubber wedges in case the floor wasn't level; a thermos of hot coffee; and most important of all, a loose-leaf notebook in which I would record the avalanche of sales I made the next day. The books I'd brought included all the multiples I'd acquired at auction last Tuesday, a selection of our own books brought from Haslemere, another selection from those friend's parents who'd died, and an even more substantial selection of the books my parents had left me. These included a number of "prize bindings" from my mother's family - thick, heavy, leather-covered tomes that had been specially bound for school prizes nearly 100 years ago and whose only literary or antiquarian value - unless one actually collected redundant self-improvement tracts such as Farrar's *Eric*, or, *Little by Little* - was that they looked magnificent lined up on a shelf. Which was why I'd brought them. As I was locking my car, two more basement dealers arrived in *their* old Volvos and began unloading boxes. They introduced themselves when they'd finished, welcomed me to Troglodytes' Bottom, and asked if I'd taken over Sam Crierly's old spot. I said I had. The one named Miggins assured me it was an excellent location, "first stall they see coming in", and the other one, who called himself Draft or Draught, seconded that promising opinion, but added, "for the basement, at least . . .", which immediately triggered a discussion (the Troglodytes' favourite, I soon learned) about every basement dweller's ambition to move to a stall upstairs in the light.

"One of us does get there occasionally," Draft or Draught assured me, "but it's trickier than you might think."

I refrained from saying I hadn't thought about it at all, actually, and simply tried to look sympathetic.

"First," said Miggins, "an upstairs stall has to become available - which doesn't happen that often . . ."

"Hen's teeth," D or D put in solemnly.

"Then Stanley has to be satisfied that you comply with his two upstairs rules: that the quality of your goods will add to the market's reputation and that the stall-holders adjacent to you are prepared to accept you as a neighbour; neither competing with, nor distracting from, their own goods." He shook his head sadly. "I've been turned down twice on distraction." (Miggins dealt in Edwardian naturist photographs). "And Geoffrey . . ." he nodded toward D or D, ". . . may never make it."

"There's a woman there, deals in antique glass, who hates me," D or D offered.

I asked him what he dealt in.

"Antique glass…" he said.

At which moment Stanley appeared at the big loading doors and we began taking our goods inside.

I'd noticed yesterday, when Ellie showed me around, that all the basement stalls were arranged with their shelves or tables flat against the walls. Practical, perhaps, but monotonous and not terribly inviting. I had decided, therefore, to arrange my shelves with two at right angles to the wall to create a sort of entrance leading to the rest of my offerings. I filled this entry bookshelf with my "prize bindings" and stepped back. *Yes, definitely eye-catching.* I priced the eye-catchers at

£30 each, (a bit under for those with less than pristine covers), not expecting anybody to buy them - unless they'd come hunting specifically for impressive bindings to display in their own bookshelves - but hoping they'd be enticed to look for more affordable prizes beyond. These I priced at £5, £10 or £15 each and arranged in my remaining bookshelves according to subject or genre - bird books in one bunch, children's picture books in a second, thrillers in a third, and so on.

After setting up I wandered around the basement to see how the other stalls compared with mine. None of those selling books – three in all - had the sort of entry I'd created, which pleased me. And several, I noted, looked rather scruffy and unloved, which pleased me even more.

"If good presentation means anything to the basement punters, I think I'm going to do all right," I told Maryanne at supper that evening - and went to bed with visions of book sales dancing in my head.

******

At six the next morning, in a driving rainstorm, I joined the merry crowd waiting outside the Bartlett Street Market for the basement doors to open. The out-of-town buyers, already numbering 100 or more, were gathered in a make-shift queue to one side protected by a canopy of brightly-coloured umbrellas. Of my 40-odd fellow stall-holders, a dozen or more, armed with blankets and plastic sheets, were crouched like mother hens over unprotected bags and boxes, hoping not to have to display dripping muslin finery or sodden cardboard boxes filled with Dinky Toys. The rest, some with umbrellas, some not, had already begun arguing about who deserved to be promoted upstairs. Listening to them I kept thinking, *What's the point?* Why waste all that energy?

But then, I was new.

******

I learned a lot in the basement during the time I toiled there: a lot about selling books; a lot about people who bought books; a lot about buying and selling in general, and a lot about myself. The first thing I learned about selling books, from the stall-holder's perspective, anyway, was the importance of a chair. Next, whether standing or sitting, was the importance of never being caught reading a newspaper. Reading a book was fine; subliminally implying diligence. Reading a newspaper suggested sloth, and worse, a cavalier attitude toward browsers. (Unless they are seeking a specific title, virtually all people who come to second-hand book stalls begin as browsers, and must be manoeuvred into becoming customers through the medium of charm - charm in stall-holders' argot being the art of successfully pretending interest in the uninteresting.)

Even more importantly, I learned that people who frequented book stalls in markets like this were looking for one thing only - bargains. If they could buy something cheaply from a stall that looked as if it were proud of its appearance, so much the better. But the key word was "cheap". And along with the regulars who came back week after week looking for 50p Len Deightons or discarded copies of *Longitude*, the most persistent of all these bargain-hunters were the runners; men, and occasionally women, who made their precarious livings buying books at bargain prices from markets and auctions, charity shops, country fairs, even from shop-lifters, I suppose, and then selling them on at a small profit to retail bookshop owners for subsequent resale. Half-a-dozen of these courageous people appeared faithfully at my stall at six each Wednesday morning, offering me books at low prices and prepared to examine every title on my shelves for bargains they could sell on elsewhere. One in particular, a man named McBride, who looked remarkably like Rolf Harris, appeared just as faithfully at Bankes Books, years later, sometimes offering me titles I'd sold to him years before. I knew McBride hadn't kept those books all that time. They'd have been sold and resold several times over before coming back to me. Still, I was moved by the sense of continuity; like the seasons coming round year after year. I was moved, too, by McBride's tenacity and unwavering good humour. The life of a runner was not one I could have sustained.

Another lesson involved the surprising number of people who came to the market each week to try to sell something to the

traders. In my case, these were mainly respectable, middle-class wom-
en, often looking a bit sheepish, asking if I would buy their husbands',
fathers' or children's long abandoned books, however small the price
might be. None ever admitted it, but I felt many were embarrassed
to approach proper bookshops with these offerings for fear they'd
be scorned as worthless. Unsurprisingly, most were worthless - I was
once actually offered a wartime cook-book full of yummy recipes for
Spam - mainly comprising stacks of grubby DIY manuals, *Readers
Digest* condensations, children's damaged pop-up storybooks, endless
annuals for Dandy or Beano or Champion - all quite unsaleable because of their condition or content. (Though I did once buy myself
a tatty old Champion annual just for the fun of revisiting the exploits
of my boyhood heroes Rockfist Rogan of the RAF, and Wilson, the
Amazing Athlete.) However hopeless, though, I always looked carefully through these offerings for sleepers. They didn't turn up often,
but twice, unbeknownst to their owners, I did discover fairy story collections illustrated by Arthur Rackham. Both were trade editions, not
deluxe firsts, but they were in good condition. I explained their value,
gave a fair price for them, and both made me a decent profit at auction later. Some of those meetings also resulted in later house calls
where I was invited to look at larger selections of books and occasionally whole libraries that were being sold. I couldn't profit greatly from
these visits while I was still dealing from the stall, but once Bankes
Books was up and running, the lessons I'd learned in patience, diplomacy and ad lib psychology from these early negotiations proved of
great benefit.

******

It was at the stall, too, about six months after I'd begun trading
there, that I first encountered the 'What if it's stolen?' question. A
charming, neatly dressed young man who called himself Andrew, appeared early one Wednesday morning with a beautifully illustrated,
eighteenth century flower book in near mint condition that he said he
needed to sell. We talked a bit while I flicked through the pages and
it emerged that his grandfather had a whole library of such books

at home. I checked in the copy of *Book Auction Records* I kept at the stall, discovered that only one copy of this book had come to auction the previous year, made Andrew a fair offer based on the sale price reached, and asked him to sign a receipt and add his address at the bottom. He did this willingly, expressing what appeared to be genuine surprise that the figure I offered was so high. I assured him it was not excessive, then asked him if he owned the book himself or was selling it for his grandfather - at which point he blushed from the top of his neck to his fair wavy hair, and I thought, *Oh oh, has Grandpa's beloved botanical collection just gone short one volume?* I learned subsequently from Grandpa himself that it was Andrew, still an undergraduate at Exeter, who'd gone short; that the flower book, given as a gift, was Grandpa's way of helping out, and that the blush resulted from simple embar-rassment. Still, the moment of frisson I'd felt on suddenly wondering if I were dealing in stolen goods, was something I never forgot - and something which stood me in good stead on several later occasions in the book shop.

******

A novice bookseller at the Wednesday market was, I discovered, a magnet for more experienced traders. In my first few weeks, I was merely surprised and rather flattered when more and more well-known dealers turned up at my stall and bought more and more of my books at what I believed were more or less competitive prices. I didn't believe it after the incident of the miniatures, though: I still cringe to remember, like a schoolboy remembering being turned down for a dance by the prettiest girl at the ball, the Wednesday morning in November when I proudly sold six beautiful, calf-bound miniature books (2x3 inches) to one of the old pros for £55 the lot, feeling terribly pleased with myself since I'd only paid a runner £5 each for them earlier that morning - only to learn from another old pro, miffed, I supposed, at not having got to me first, that my six little books were in fact worth £60 each. I swallowed my pride and told Peter the story that same afternoon: "I suddenly felt like a baby rabbit cornered by predatory hawks," I confessed. He told me not to worry

about it, said the lesson learned was worth the few pounds lost, and
assured me that all newcomers were given the raptor treatment their
first few months in the market.

"It's that kind of business," he said. "We're all gentlemen, and
we're all terribly honourable. But when it's among ourselves, it really
is raptors and rabbits. And once you know how to handle that, it gets
to be rather fun."

Only two weeks later, and despite Peter's cautionary advice, I became the victim of another predator (who, in fairness, was only doing
his job) when I priced a three volume early edition of Jane Austen in
original publisher's green cloth at £100. I had bought the books from
two charming old ladies at a charity fête in a village outside Bath,
who were raising money for a school in East Africa. They were asking
£50 and I paid them that happily, quite innocently ignorant of the
fact that the Austen set would have attracted £500-£600 at any respectable auction. No sooner had I placed the books prominently on
display the following Wednesday morning, than a tall, clerical-look-
ing gentleman wearing steel granny-specs (a dealer, obviously, straight
out of Trollope) began examining each volume with considerable interest, but also with what appeared to be considerable disappointment judging from the "Tut tuts" and "Oh, dears" I kept hearing as
he turned over pages.

"What's your best price on these?" he asked finally.

"£90," I answered, trying to sound firm.

"No, no," he said, contemptuously, "I mean your very best price.
I am Greenson."

*Greenson? Oh, Lord, was this some trade password I didn't know? Some
terrifying Masonic open-sesame?*

"Well, I could do them for £80, I suppose." (*Fool* - I should have
said, "My very best price? £120.")

"£70," he said, and I, retiring weakly, sighed, "Oh, all right
then."

That was the last of my seriously cringe-making apprenticeship
gaffes. And in fact, I don't think I ever sold anything for less than I'd
paid for it. But I do remember too many books sold for far less than
they should have fetched in those early days, which was a personal

disappointment, I suppose, but one with a positive side as well. To keep the stall up to the high aesthetic standard I'd set for it, I bought scores of multiple trays of often scruffy-looking leather-bound books, cleaned them up, checked their recent auction prices, and offered them as single items. I never pulled off a fantastic coup this way, but I was able to make a small profit from each sale and in the process built a reputation for always having interesting books on offer at not too exorbitant prices.

******

Opposite my stall were Pauline and Dave who dealt in general antiques, but whose specialty was clocks. Dave was clearly something of a genius at clock-repairing, and every Wednesday morning he had a wide clientele bringing him all sorts of odd-looking timepieces for mending. Whenever the job was not too complicated, he would dismantle and repair a clock right there on the long table that fronted their stall. This naturally brought lots of people around to watch, and not infrequently, to buy. Which was the point, of course. Pauline and Dave also knew the value of a smile, and their stall, when busy, was always a cheerful, sunny place despite being underground. When there were no customers, though, the smiles disappeared and the two of them embarked on the usual stall-holder pastime of complaining about business, the weather, the economy, the cheap-skate customers and being stuck in a cavern like moles. Dave played the chirpy Cockney sparrow when there was an audience of potential buyers, talking non-stop as he praised the quite unique features of the perfectly ordinary carriage clock he was holding aloft. Pauline had a different sales technique: getting the clock (or copper bedpan or whatever it was) into the customer's hands as quickly as possible, and then evading specific questions such as, "Is this really Georgian?" with say, "It was sold to me as Georgian," or "Unless I've been badly fooled," when she knew perfectly well whatever it was had been made in Taiwan in 1980, then rubbed with shoe polish and grit to make it look old (called 'distressing', a perfectly legitimate practice in the antiques trade at market level). Dave clearly derived professional satisfaction from

believing his Pearly King routine was what clinched the sales he made.
Pauline derived her satisfaction wholly from the acquisition of cash.

Both had been a little wary of me when I first moved in across
from them, fearing, perhaps, that their customers would abandon
their Georgian clocks and antique warming pans for the irresistible
lure of a 1950 Guinness Book of Records or a Cornish poetry an-
thology. They soon became friendly, though, and even quite helpful. They'd recently had a £150 cheque bounce (each assuming the
other had been too trusting) and volunteered the invaluable advice
that I should only take payment in cash for book sales under about
£50, and fix myself up with a credit card facility as soon as possible
for larger deals. I began making arrangements the very next day; by
the following Wednesday I was ready to swipe away with the best of
them.

At that time, different credit card companies charged different
percentages for each transaction made, and again following Pauline
and Dave's advice, I excluded the one card whose percentage rate
was absurdly higher than any of the others. I continued that practice
throughout my years in the shop, and only once lost a sale because the
buyer carried only that card. The £1300 lost did not make me happy,
but I wasn't disheartened for long - it turned out the buyer was a con
man and the card had been stolen.

Another thing I learned from them, was the importance of regularly surveying my stall from the customer's point of view. Dave would
actually walk past his two or three times in a morning, to see what
might lure him in as a customer. With his stock, he said, it was mainly
novelty. With mine, I decided, it was style and the sense of discovering
something new. Books with attractive or amusing dust wrappers were
good for this, so were double-page engravings. I learnt, too, that if my
display remained the same as it had been the previous week, fewer
visitors would stop to browse. No mystery, really. Regulars were the
mainstays of the Wednesday markets, and if a display wasn't reborn
each week, the natural response would be, "same old stuff, no point
stopping."

I rarely encountered Pauline and Dave after leaving the market,
but whenever I thought of them it was always with gratitude for their

friendliness, their willingness to watch my stall when I went upstairs for a coffee or breakfast (I did the same for them), and the excellent advice they gave me.

Another stall-holder I remember with fondness was Haydon. Gentle and quiet, Haydon was an artist fallen on hard times. He wore a long, dusty brown overcoat and a wide black fedora that were familiar sights on the Bath antique circuit. At the Wednesday market, he showed portrait sketches of unrecognizable people and small, badly framed watercolour scenes of the Bath countryside, also mostly unrecognizable. He normally arrived in a cheerful mood with Lucy, his Dalmatian, on a rope lead at his heels, scratching the floor with her unclipped nails. But one Wednesday morning, he came past my stall looking seriously gloomy, and explained that he hadn't enough money to feed Lucy, let alone himself. He opened his stall, convinced that things would turn around for them today. When I saw them again at lunch time - it was obvious they hadn't. "Taking Lucy out for a walk," he said, still looking gloomy, and came back ten minutes later looking even gloomier, though Lucy, at least, looked somewhat relieved. Then an hour or so later, an obnoxious looking German tourist in a Tyrolean hat with a shaving brush stuck in the band and a bright blue bandana tied around his fat neck, came waddling into the basement and made his way pompously along the aisle between stalls, pausing here and there to tell a stall holder that his 'junk' was 'ridiculously overpriced' or another that he had no right to insult the public by offering such laughable rubbish. When he got to Haydon's stall, he stopped short, drew himself up superciliously, looked at everything on display, then said loudly:

"How much the dog?"

A sharp intake of breath went round the market. We all waited.

"Fifty Pounds," said Haydon, finally. (*At least he hadn't said a fiver.*)

"I take," said the German, handed over a £50 note, and out he went with Lucy on her rope behind him.

Sad to see her go, but good to know that Haydon would surely sup well that night.

A regular visitor to my stall was a tall, ruddy young man called Hugo, who claimed he had recently resigned a fellowship at an American University, to take a up a place in the English Department at Reading. Hugo was very knowledgeable indeed about books and would tell me - and the whole basement - everything worth knowing about any book I might be showing on the stall - or any book at all, for that matter. He had a deep, sonorous voice which echoed and re-echoed alarmingly around the walls with the annoying ring of self-satisfaction. I asked him once if he would mind whispering, which he good-naturedly did, but somehow his whispers were no less audible than his normal voice and hence no less annoying. Several dealers told me he was well known at book fairs and fêtes for picking up a book, telling the stall-holder everything about it, then putting it back and walking away trilling Purcell or Orlando Gibbon at the top of his voice. Booksellers tended to fade from view when they saw him coming, but nothing, it seems, could dampen his astonishing good humour and smugness. At the Wednesday market he would frequently pull a book from my shelves, glance at its price, tell me it was far too cheap and inform me that I should be charging twice as much for it at least. I would remind him that this was a market, not a major London bookseller, and that my intention was to sell the book at a small profit before the day was out. "Much too cheap, dear boy, much too cheap," he would keep insisting. Which was doubly annoying considering it was known that Hugo never spent more than £35 for a second-hand book, and that even parting with £30 made him most uneasy. Something, the basement dwellers all agreed, had to be done about this man. And late one Wednesday morning in November, the moment of reckoning arrived. Hugo spotted a charming three-volume duodecimo set of Percy's *Reliques* that I'd marked at £50 - which was an absurdly generous price, and we both knew it.

"Usual discount?" he asked.

"Yes, of course - £45."

Then, at full volume, using everything from charm, to pleading, to reminders of all the help he'd given me in the past, Hugo set about trying to argue me down to £35. I let him make enough progress, one pound at a time, to think he might actually succeed - then at

£40, I stuck. Twice he walked away. Twice he came back. Eventually, close to weeping, he dragged two £20 notes from his pocket and
allowed me to prise them from his fingers. To the credit of my fellow
stall-holders there were no cheers or cat-calls - just a polite smattering
of applause. Which to Hugo's credit, he acknowledged with a deep
theatrical bow, before withdrawing from the field humming a lesser
known madrigal by William Byrd.

******

One morning shortly after the Hugo incident, Ellie came down
to whisper that a stall upstairs would be available starting the following Wednesday and to ask if I would like it. I learned later that
this rare honour had come my way because the empty space stood
next to the very dealer in antique glass who had been keeping poor
D or D imprisoned down here since before I'd first arrived. In fact,
this woman had been vetoing everyone on grounds of competition or
distraction since she'd moved upstairs herself nearly four years previously, and had only consented to my moving in because a tidy, polite
bookstall might actually attract the right sort of spill-over custom to
her stall. But more importantly, she agreed because there was talk of
Stanley, who was not above taking a bribe if it were large enough,
moving a dealer selling novelty robots into the neighbouring slot
whether the glass dealer agreed or not. I felt a bit of a traitor to D or
D saying yes to Ellie, but I wasn't about to turn down the offer of light
on grounds of anything as ridiculous as principle. So, the following
Tuesday afternoon I moved everything upstairs with the expectation
of meeting an altogether finer (all right - richer) class of customer. As
it turned out, all my basement customers simply followed me upstairs
and hardly anyone new visited the stall for about three weeks. Then
gradually they began to appear - customers not necessarily finer in
discernment, education or social grace, but (as I'd shamefully hoped),
customers with fuller wallets. They were the Christmas, birthday, and
wedding present crowd; the buyers of graduation gifts for nephews
and godchildren; the generous aunts and uncles who didn't at all
mind being asked by me how much they wanted to spend, and even

knew the sorts of things the future recipients of their largesse might
like.

    With the arrival of this new clientele, the entries in my notebook
of sales began to multiply. My weekly takings grew larger and larger.
The old pros who had fleeced me mercilessly a year before now came
to me for advice about the correct price for a certain edition of a
certain book they were a bit uncertain about.

                                    ******

    After fourteen months in the market, eleven in the basement and
three upstairs, I'd settled into a comfortable, easy-to-manage work
routine - selling at the stall each Wednesday, then spending the rest
of my week buying at auctions, book fairs and the occasional private
house when invited. I was also offered books by other stall-holders
now, sometimes quite good ones they'd picked up in mixed lots at
house clearances or in charity sales. I bought from the runners, too,
but not often; we were both in the same business, after all, and our
potential profit margins were nearly identical. As the months went by,
though, I deliberately bought more and more books from my regular
customers - and always at generous prices - not because I expected to
make more from them now I'd moved upstairs, but because I was already planning ahead for the day when I had a shop of my own. The
habit of "taking books to Mr. Bankes" would have become automatic
for them, thus providing me with both a loyal customer base and a
ready source of new stock.

    Then, on the eve of my fifteenth month at the market, while
having coffee with Peter Goodden before a Tuesday auction, I had
what I suppose people call an epiphany: It was an icy cold morning in November. Peter was talking about a poetry collection he was
hoping to get. I was gazing across the street at a strange painting of
irises in the Adam Gallery's window while I listened. All at once a
handsome, middle-aged woman wearing a splendid red coat hurried
past in the direction of Bath Brown's with an auction catalogue in
her arms - and for no apparent reason it suddenly struck me that
I'd actually begun to think, and act, and do business like a proper

bookseller. I seemed to know now what to do and what not to do. Seemed to know whom I could trust and whom I couldn't. Seemed to have created, without noticing, a reputation for honesty, cheerfulness and knowledgeability among my colleagues and customers. Seemed to feel confident bidding at auctions. And thanks to my apprenticeship in the market, seemed to know instinctively how to evaluate, collate, prepare, and display books. Seeing that woman, I felt sure all at once that I could make a good living at this business, and that the sooner I had my own shop, the sooner that living would become even better.

Then early the very next day, that same woman wearing the same red coat, materialised at the stall, introduced herself, and said, "I've searched every bookshop in Bath, Mr. Bankes. None could help me, but nearly all of them suggested I come to you. So here I am."

"What can I do?" I said.

"Do you know my cat Jeoffry?" she asked.

Any other trader in the building would have replied, "Why, is he lost?"

What I said was, "Would that be the cat who is the servant of the living God?"

"It would, indeed," she said, and beamed.

"And let me guess - would you be looking for a copy of the *Jubilate Agno*?"

"I would," she said, still beaming. "An early edition, even a first if such things still exist, nicely bound and in top notch condition, and signed, ideally, by Mr. Smart."

"A gift?"

"For my husband's sixtieth."

"Money no object?"

"Within reason," she smiled.

I quoted her a theoretical price - ballpark, as the Americans say.

"That would be fine," she said. "Can you find one for me?"

"I believe I just might," I said.

We exchanged contact information, she shook hands again, wished me good hunting, started to walk away - then turned around and came back.

"May I ask you one more question, Mr. Bankes?"

"Of course you may."

"Do forgive me if I'm being impertinent, but I'd have thought you'd have your own bookshop…"

******

"Positively Sibylline," Maryanne said, when I told her the story that evening.

"Exactly what I thought," I said.

"I shall start looking for a shop at once," she smiled.

CHAPTER THREE: THE BOOKSHOP

*"The proprietor should
avoid taking lunch at his desk."*

Recently, while clearing out cupboards at the Brock Street flat,
Sarah came across a list of "Do's and Don'ts for the ideal bookshop"
that Maryanne and I had compiled after supper that very same November evening more than 20 years ago. Our rules were based pri-
marily on what we agreed discerning customers would want to see on
entering Bankes Books, and began:

- The shop must always look clean and tidy, even if it means going in early every morning to vacuum. (Curses!)
- The proprietor (me) must also always look clean and tidy. (More
curses!)
- The proprietor's desk must not be littered with newspapers, utility bills, invoices, accounting ledgers, shopping lists, scribbly notes,
grandchildren's toys, or books that are in any way tatty. A few attractive, leather-bound volumes nicely arranged would be acceptable,
and one would also have a telephone, credit card machine, and desk

lamp. But that is all.

- Coffee mugs must never be seen standing about - especially half-empty ones.

- Any drink consumed by the proprietor must be taken from a horrid little plastic cup: two gulps and into the wastepaper bin immediately.

- As a general rule, the proprietor should avoid taking lunch at his desk; this rule to be applied especially to sandwich lunches where bits of egg-salad, sliced tomatoes, cheese crumbs, pickles, or (God forbid!) oily Greek olives (my favourite) risked staining a priceless sixteenth century page. Instead, the proprietor should lunch modestly at one of Bath's better restaurants - avoiding fried foods, rich puddings and garlic.

- Whenever the proprietor goes out he must carefully lock up and hang an open/closed sign on the shop door stating the exact time of his return.

- If the proprietor must lunch on the premises (especially where sandwiches are involved), he must do so out-of-sight, (e.g. behind furniture) so that people passing the shop cannot see him spilling pickled beetroot down his shirt.

- Good paintings and engravings from Maryanne's family should hang on any wall not covered by a display shelf.

(Later these would be superseded by the splendid fine art prints Sarah began showing in one corner of the shop some years after her remarriage to the estimable Jim Heavens, Home Office whiz-kid and renowned amateur actor - of which and whom more later).

- Whatever the cost, there must be a very good carpet on the floor.

- There should also be two, but only two, handsome, well upholstered armchairs standing in quiet corners beyond the proprietor's desk.

- A butler's tray on folding legs should be located just outside the shop entrance piled with entertaining, un-scruffy paperbacks suitable for holiday reading. Browsers who wished to purchase any of these would have to enter the shop to pay, and might then be directed to other, more expensive books . . .

Our list of rules ran on to nearly three pages, and as I recall, when we'd finished compiling it at half-past ten that evening, we decided, with no little sense of satisfaction, that the really hard work had more or less been done. All that remained now was to find and acquire a suitable shop, decorate and furnish it, move the stock in and start doing business. That, we thought, would not be especially easy.

******

Except, as it turned out, finding the right shop was easy. Within two weeks of making that list, following half-a-dozen disappointments at the hands of estate agents, Maryanne found the perfect premises, quite by accident, in what was for me the most ideal location imaginable. She was having her hair done one morning in a salon in Margarets Buildings, (the pedestrianised shopping street that runs north between Brock Street and Catherine Place). As she was leaving, the proprietor, who knew we were looking for a commercial location, took her aside, confided that she was selling her lease and moving to Jamaica with her boyfriend - and wondered if Maryanne might be interested? (In the lease, not a threesome in Jamaica.)

"The lease looks quite reasonable," Maryanne told me at dinner that night. "Howard (our solicitor) thought so, too. Fair rent, break clauses at twelve and sixteen years; otherwise, the only stipulations are to carry adequate insurance, keep the place looking decent and hand it back in good condition when we leave."

"When can I see it?"

"Tomorrow morning," Maryanne said, and held up some keys on a velvet ribbon.

The shop comprised ground floor and basement, so there was plenty of space. Plenty of light, too, with a big bow window looking out onto Margarets Buildings and another big window at the back. The shop was set back about six feet from the street on a slightly raised pavement, which created a sort of covered porch, gave it a cosy, almost picture-book feel, and meant there was plenty of room for my butler's tray of tempting holiday paperbacks. Downstairs, there was a back door leading into the big parking area behind the Buildings for bringing in stock. There was a paper shop on the corner where I could pick up a *Times*; a good deli three doors along toward Catherine Place where I could pick up illicit nibbles, and a bar restaurant across from the deli called the Vendange, where I could have a good lunch at a modest price and pick up all the local gossip from Shaw, the beguiling ex-head mistress who ran the place. But of all its many virtues, the best thing about the brand new Bankes Books was that I could get to it each morning in under three minutes by simply walking out of our front door and crossing Brock Street.

******

We celebrated signing the lease with dinner at the Royal Crescent Hotel that evening, and first thing the next morning, the decorators moved in - the decorators being Maryanne, Sarah, Nicholas and I.

Nicholas, who has a natural gift for turning ordinary-looking space into striking-looking space, (he now does that for a world-renowned British retailer), took responsibility for bookshelves, tables, occasional furniture and "getting the ambience right". Maryanne, who assured me again that the two most important things in a bookshop were lighting and carpeting, took on the sourcing and purchasing of those, plus choosing curtains, selecting paint colours, hanging paintings and prints when the time came, and in general overseeing decisions about taste. (The carpet she chose, a dark green cord which looked staggeringly expensive - and was - lasted the whole twenty years we had the shop without betraying a single sign that anyone had ever trodden on it.) Sarah handled paper-work, errands, and arranging for plumbers, electricians, handymen and part time body-builders when needed for heavy work, while I concentrated on a what-to-show-where plan for both floors, plus organising and packing the books ready for moving into the shop. Once all the hairdressing gear had been removed and the walls stripped and primed, Sarah and Nicholas repainted the place - two coats upstairs and down, walls, window frames, woodwork and ceilings in just eight days. While they were doing that, professional decorators completed outside repairs and painted the front of the shop a dark, elegant forest green. The new lighting went in next, then the carpet, then the book shelves Nicholas had had built - tall, handsome, finely made objects of walnut and oak, two of them standing on an old long table (made for the nursery at Haslemere) against one long wall so that their tops just reached the ceiling. "Good visual effect", he assured me, and it was.

He arranged the rest of the shelves, ten in all, standing on the floor at various locations around the room to create the appearance of alcoves, then located my desk and fine leather swivel chair right by the door - "Where you can keep an eye on thieves," Sarah said, solemnly.

"There won't be thieves, will there?" I said, in mock horror.

"Of course there will, Dad. Who ever heard of a smart antiquarian bookshop without thieves?"

"Smart, do you think? Really?"

"Definitely," Sarah said. "They'll be queuing up to steal your Trollopes."

We moved another dozen lesser shelves into the two rooms downstairs, cleaned up and painted the little bathroom near the outside door, brought in a second desk and swivel chair (plus extension telephone, card machine, et al) for when I had customers down there, put up several colourful posters for decoration, and all at once we had a quite lively-looking bargain basement for the economy-minded browser.

Upstairs, of course, was where I would display the rare seventeenth and eighteenth century books, the early Dickens and Popes, and others liable to be stolen - with the rarest and most expensive of them displayed in glass-fronted cabinets behind my desk, or on a table right beside it where they couldn't be got at without shifting me. (No mean feat, that, shifting a 6-foot-3-inch, 17 stone teddy bear who is disinclined to be shifted by much of anything, anyway.) Titles would be displayed together by subject or kind - travel, poetry, art, philosophy, religion, modern firsts, fine sets, good bindings, Bibles, children's books, and so on. Downstairs, would be like my market stall in Bartlett Street crammed with as many different kinds of books as its dozen shelves could hold; all jumbled together with only a polite gesture toward logic. Upstairs, I pictured as being orderly, rich, quietly sumptuous, like a reading room in a club in St. James's.

Downstairs would be a sort of Aladdin's Cave, complete with a £2 section, where one would immediately feel, on descending from above, that treats would surely be found if one looked long enough: the ideal birthday or Christmas present, something special for under a tenner to present to a host as thanks for a week-end stay, or that elusive, second-hand *Cowper Powys* one had been looking for for ages. Together, the two floors would make just the sort of bookshop I imagined people would enjoy coming to - (once word of mouth had done its job as Publicity Manager) - as well as just the sort of bookshop I would be proud to say I owned. Even if everyone did think I was called Mr. Bankes.

The day after we finished furnishing the downstairs sale room, the insurance company sent a man from a firm called ShopGard to install a new burglar alarm. It had an elaborate control panel fixed just inside the shop door, and a big white alarm box high up on the outside wall with lights that flashed day and night, and a whooping siren that would waken sleeping neighbours three streets away. Pointless, really, since no respectable burglar would ever bother breaking into a shop like ours where he had no idea what was and wasn't worth stealing, or where to sell it afterwards if he did get lucky, except to someone like me, or another rare bookdealer, which would lead immediately to his arrest, of course. Still, the insurance company insisted, so I learned the buttons and signed a direct debit order for the rental on the damned thing. Then, as Mr. ShopGard was packing up, I asked politely if he had any gadgets for deterring shop-lifters.

"Don't be ridiculous," he said, cheerfully, and left.

In all the years we had the shop, no one ever tried to break in after hours. (A tribute to the burglar alarm's presence? I seriously doubt it.) Shop-lifting, on the other hand, as Sarah had worried, was a constant problem. And while precautions could be taken - (never trust a browser on a hot summer's day wearing a large mac) - I had to recognise that a determined book-lifter, perhaps needing £10 or £20 for a fix - or milk for the baby - would always manage to get away with something. Curiously, though, I gradually came to understand that it was rarely the taking of a valuable book that distressed me as much as the taking of perhaps a quite ordinary one that had a story attached to it: There was a Keats, for example, worth about £20, part of a small library I'd driven miles to value. It was owned by a charming old woman who lived alone in a cottage in Herefordshire with an ancient orange cat she called Black and White because her grandson's favourite TV show was Postman Pat. I really did hate having that book stolen, and only hope the thief found some joy from what he got for it.

The last piece of furniture we moved into the shop before opening was a magnificent eighteenth century, open-handed, long case clock from Maryanne's family house in Lancashire. We placed it at the end of a bookcase facing the entry, where it immediately took on the character of a tall, well-dressed, utterly reliable old friend. I never wound the chime for fear of damaging it; but the clock's sonorous ticking somehow made the shop feel cosy and warm even when it was freezing out and no one was there except me. Over the years, a number of customers inquired if the clock were for sale. And occasionally, quite tempting sums were mentioned, but I always said no. The clock wasn't mine, for a start, and besides one does not sell an old friend.

"Splendid," Sarah said, as we stood back to admire it.

"Perfect," said Maryanne.

"The shop's ready to go, Dad," Nicholas declared.

"Except for one thing," I reminded them . . .

*****

And at dawn the next morning we started moving in the books. When I say "we", I mean Sarah and me carrying the lighter boxes and two rugby second-row forwards we'd hired carrying the heavier ones from Brock Street across to the shop. Unlike a house move where a reasonably-sized library of 500-600 books might fill 25-30 boxes, mine numbered 5000 and filled 400 boxes; a few of them weighing as much as 60 pounds when packed, the rest rarely less than 30. (The heaviest certainly more than a willowy daughter and an ageing stuffed animal could reasonably handle, we felt, without incurring chiropractic bills - hence the rugby players.) Three weeks earlier, I'd provided myself with 1000, double card, fold-flat, packing boxes, at £1 each. Storing them later was troublesome, but they lasted as long as Bankes Books did and were a great bargain despite that inconvenience. So while Maryanne and the children were busy redecorating the shop, I spent most of my time underground preparing and packing books. Those destined for the upstairs room in the shop, because of their expensive, often delicate bindings, I kept to under 30 per box, (thickness of book dictating the exact number), placed in line on edge, spine downwards, so that they fitted snugly without squeezing or scraping covers. (For booksellers there are few things more discouraging than unpacking a box of expensive titles packed by someone who is not a bookseller, and discovering three shredded dust-wrappers and a bent board.) Books for the downstairs room required less careful packing, but still had to be packed safely. I labelled each box with a description of its contents - geographical, nineteenth century fiction, atlases etc. - and a letter "U" for upstairs, "D" for down, so it could be deposited nearish to the appropriate shelf when delivered to the shop. I also double-checked that multiple sets (a complete Shakespeare, for example, presented in individual calf-bound volumes) were all together in the same box. (One of the other really discouraging things when making a move like this: discovering on unpacking that all the plays are there except *Coriolanus*, or *Timon*, and then having fretted for hours over how much one had lost on that deal, coming upon the damned thing tucked in amongst the Jane Austens for no apparent reason.) Finally, knowing we had a long day ahead of us, we got a good supply of food and drink together in the Brock Street kitchen for the team; lager, soft drinks, crisps, sandwich makings, pizzas to warm in the oven, then telephoned the rugby players to let them know D-Day was at hand.

Operations began at 7 a.m. the next morning. The last box was delivered at 4 p.m., and at 10 that night, as Nicholas and I folded down the last of the empty boxes and carried them into the basement, Maryanne and Sarah slid the last two books into their places on the last two shelves - and just like that we had a bookshop!

The Opening

After a discussion that lasted at most 30 seconds, we decided quite happily not to have one. Instead, we thought I should simply go over to the shop the next day, prepare it for business, sit down at my desk and see what happened. This sounded just right to me since I was already imagining clamouring mobs waiting at the door when I arrived. So the next morning at seven-thirty, I walked across to Bankes Books, unlocked the front door, shut off the burglar alarm, opened the curtains, hoovered the new carpet (a bit), went down to the basement for our brand-new shopkeeper's light-weight aluminium step-ladder, carried it back upstairs and out onto the porch, went back inside for the sign we'd had painted - BANKES BOOKS, it read, in gold letters (Bodini bold, upper case) on a lacquer green board - carried it up the ladder, hung it on the wrought iron arm we'd had fixed to the wall above the shop's front door, climbed back down, put the ladder away in the basement, came back upstairs, arranged the books we'd decided on as our first display for the front window: a collection of world classics, some prize bindings and some books about Bath, carried my butler's tray of paperbacks outside, looked at my watch, (10 minutes past 8) . . . then remembering Dave from the Stanley market, walked a few steps away down Margarets Buildings and turned around for a look.

Splendid, I thought. Just the sort of bookshop I'd have wanted to own myself - if it hadn't been mine already . . .

At which point Maryanne appeared to say that a man from the *Bath Chronicle* would be turning up at nine to take photographs.

"How does the *Bath Chronicle* know about my new shop?"

"Grapevine," Maryanne said.

"What grapevine?"

"The one that knows about your new shop."

"I'll bet Peter Goodden . . . " I started to say.

At which point Peter, himself, appeared around the corner from Brock Street wearing a silly paper hat and carrying a bottle of Buck's Fizz. Sarah and Nicholas arrived from the other direction carrying another bottle. Then came Nicholas's lovely new wife, Victoria,

carrying a vast bundle of yellow roses in her arms. Then Shaw from
the Vendange came down Margarets Buildings carrying some wine
glasses- and within ten minutes, following the arrival of several more
of our shop-keeping neighbours - Julia from the launderette next
door, Carolyn and Brian from the amazing antique-cum-junk shop
three doors along, Jason Beal who sold prints and watercolours up
at the corner, the other Bryan from the paper shop, plus Draft or
Draught from the Wednesday market, followed by my faithful runner friend who looked like Rolf Harris - and all at once a kind of
impromptu, non-opening street celebration had materialised out of
nothing. And all before nine o'clock in the morning.

"Speech!" someone called out - a bit dutifully I thought, but I
gave one anyway, very briefly, saying thanks to them all for welcoming
me to the Buildings so generously, and if they didn't all immediately
dash inside and buy lots of books I'd never speak to them again . . .

Whereupon there appeared at my elbow a man so bizarrely
dressed I thought he must be a hired entertainer Nicholas had engaged as a silly joke. In fact, he was merely an American.

"Are you the owner of this shop?" he asked (pronouncing it
"shap").

"Yes, I am."

"Would you sell me this book?" he said, gave me an odd wink,
and held up a copy of *The Call of the Wild* that he must just have
picked up from the butler's tray.

"I'd be happy to sell you that book," I said, and led him inside to
my desk.

I took his two pounds, put his book in one of our new Bankes
Books carrier bags - bottle green with extra strong handles and no
writing. (We'd decided, after serious discussion, that writing on bags,
like paid publicity, was not for us.)

"Excellent holiday read," I said, handing him his purchase. "Very
exciting," and then asked him if he had always been a Jack London
fan.

"That won't be his real name," he said, lowering his voice.

"I think you'll find it is, actually."

"Mm mm," he insisted, "They never use their real names,"

and headed for the door. As he stepped outside all my neighbourly well-wishers gave him a hearty hurrah. He waved his green bag aloft in acknowledgment, did a quick leprechaun dance step, and disappeared down Margarets Buildings, never to be seen again.

"Good Lord!" I said to Maryanne, "He thinks *The Call of the Wild* is pornography."

"Doesn't matter," she replied. "That man was your first customer."

******

Too true, I was thinking ten minutes later, not hugely encouraged by the fact, as I watched Maryanne and the children walk back toward Brock Street. It was half past nine now. My welcoming committee had all dispersed back to their own shops and pursuits. Out beyond my irresistible display window, Margarets Buildings was deserted. I sat down in my dark green, butter-soft, leather swivel chair behind my clearly important, richly glowing, antiquarian bookseller's desk - feeling utterly REJECTED.

Here I was with a fine new shop, as good as a shop could be, a shop full of amazing treats and treasures that was bustling with NO CUSTOMERS AT ALL! And customers, after all, were the main point of a shop, weren't they? The *only* point in fact, as I saw it. It wasn't as if my new shop thought of itself as exclusive, or superior. I hadn't put up a sign saying, 'Well-dressed Customers Only', or 'No Bald Customers, Please', or 'Customers Who Think Jack London Writes Porn Need Not Enter'. Here at Bankes Books it was 'All Customers Welcome'. Except there wasn't a solitary one in sight for me to be welcoming to . . .

Whereupon the Right Hon. William Rees-Mogg by then, in fact, Lord Rees-Mogg, stuck his head in the door and said: "I'd hoped to have been your first customer, but I met Maryanne at the bottom of Margarets buildings and she said some silly American got in ahead of me and ruined your morning!"

"Now fully restored by you," I said, instantly bucking up.

"Thank God," he said. "Nothing worse than a ruined morning. Incidentally, there's a newspaper chap lurking outside with a camera."

(Rees-Mogg, among many things, had been editor of *The Times* for nine years, and would certainly have known a lurking journalist if he saw one.) "And your family are on their way," he continued, "and I've got to be somewhere, so,"

"So . . . ?"

"Show me your Popes, please - your very earliest."

I did, but not expecting him to find one he didn't already have in his own library. He was, among many other things, a considerable amateur Pope expert. But in fact, he did find one he wanted - a 1729 *Dunciad Variorum* incorporating the notorious preface by Scribluris - which he said he did have at home but wanted a second copy to give to his son Jacob as a birthday present. So having felt utterly rejected not a quarter of an hour earlier, I'd suddenly been visited by an old friend, made my first proper sale at Bankes Books, and during a chat of barely five minutes had learned three new things about Alexander Pope that I'd never heard before!

And all before ten o'clock in the morning!

******

A photograph of my beautiful daughter, smiling beside Victoria's lovely yellow flowers and framed by some of my most impressive bindings, appeared in *The Bath Chronicle* two days later. And while I never quite believed in the connection, I seem to recall that from then on there was rarely a moment when I didn't have at least one customer, or browser, or runner, or friend in the shop between ten o'clock in the morning when we opened and closing time at five-thirty. In business terms, as with all shops, there were good days and slow days, amazing days and dire days, days when everyone who came in seemed to be in robust good humour, and days when everybody was grumpy. But regardless of the zeitgeist, or the weather, or the state of the Nation's economy (which was never good), or the state of our sometimes mercurial bank balance, I gradually came to realise that it was the different kinds of people who came in each day that gave me the greatest satisfaction in having taken up this new life.

I can't pretend I felt grateful to the thieving swine who'd made it necessary. But at the end of a particularly good day in the shop, or following a good meal and a quiet stroll around the Royal Crescent with Maryanne on a splendid summer's evening, I sometimes did grudgingly admit to myself that the thieving swine had, quite unwittingly, done us a good turn of sorts.

CHAPTER FOUR: DRAMATIS PERSONAE

"I looked up and saw a very large black straw hat."

There was, of course, no such thing as a typical Bankes Books customer. They came in all sizes, ages, nationalities, types, and degrees of celebrity or anonymity; their backgrounds appeared to embrace the whole of the UK's and, to some extent the world's social fabric. In truth, the only two things I can say about their number generally, is that they all shared a love of books, and that with the rarest of exceptions, they were all people I liked.

Among the celebrated, I especially enjoyed the visits of James Lees-Milne, the architectural historian and biographer, who was for many years secretary of the Country House committee of the National Trust, and who in that capacity, was instrumental in saving many of Britain's finest stately homes through negotiating transfer to the Trust of their ownership from the families who could no longer afford to keep them up. Lees-Milne had retired from the Trust and lived near Tetbury at the time I started the shop, but his work as curator of the Beckford Library, which was housed at Number 20 Lansdown Crescent, brought him to Bath most days. I would often see him walk past the shop at around lunchtime - tall, and very thin, with fluffy white hair that blew in the breeze. He would almost always pause to look at the new display of books in the window, and one day he came in to ask the price of an early railway history, *The Iron Road*. I told him it was £35, to which he said at once, "Oh, dear, such a lot of money - but I ought to have it, don't you think?"

I explained that there was a special discount for anyone who signed our Visitor's Book, and that £30 plus a signature made this a quite good buy. Thereafter he visited the shop regularly, occasionally to ask if I could find a particular title for him, but mostly just to enjoy a chat about some book he'd noticed in the window or some amusing fact he'd come upon in the Beckford collection. He was always delightful to talk to, and if Maryanne happened to be there he especially enjoyed talking to her about Winstanley, (alas, a stately home the Trust was unable to rescue).

We visited Lees-Milne's home, (one of the gate houses at Badminton), where we saw his own collection of beautifully cared for and polished books; and in his bedroom, a bookcase holding a number of the books which formed part of the William Beckford library that he looked after. (Beckford, aesthete par excellence, built both Fonthill Abbey to house his own art collection along with Edward Gibbon's enormous library which he purchased in the 1790's, and the splendid Beckford Tower on the hill just north of Bath, that now serves as a museum housing many of the treasures he accumulated.) He is believed to have been the richest commoner in England in the later eighteenth century (his fortune, inherited from his father, who was twice Lord Mayor of London, derived, as did many fortunes in that era, from sugar and slaves). He was a musician, poet, bibliophile, amateur historian, and quite possibly Bath's most important cultural benefactor.

Lees-Milne was justifiably proud of having been made caretaker of William Beckford's splendid library; but one day, almost with tears in his bright blue eyes, he came into the shop to say that he'd done a dreadful thing for which he felt he could never forgive himself. He had, he explained, given a number of the Beckford books we'd seen at his home to the Bath Heritage Trust, who, along with administering No.1 Royal Crescent, had responsibility for the upkeep and care of

Beckford's Tower.

Misunderstanding his distress, I tried to console him by saying that absent books could be fondly thought of as absent friends; sadly gone, but still alive in one's memory.

"No, no, it's not that," he said. "It's that they'll be shoved into a cupboard somewhere and won't ever again be seen by the people who love them. Or, worse, that the heritage people, because they're so chronically short of money, will feel they need to sell them."

Legally speaking, they had every right to do just that. And sure enough, the very next day, the Chairman of the Bath Heritage Trust looked into the shop to ask if I could come round to Number 1 that evening and do a valuation of some Beckford books the Trust had just been given. I did go round, of course, and in a very short time was relieved to be able to disappoint him with news that none of the books he'd been given was worth anywhere near the £20-25 thousand he'd hoped for. In perfect order, a number of them would have fetched that. But 250 years ago, when it was normal practice for a gentleman to have his books rebound to suit the style of his library, the eccentric Mr. Beckford - for whom the resale value of a book he loved would have held no interest at all - had the engaging, typically daft habit of instructing Charles Lewis, his binder, to interleave each book with blank sheets of paper so that he could write notes about the original text as observations occurred to him. A splendid scheme for a bibliophile bursting with ideas and unlimited funds - less splendid for an underfunded heritage organisation trying to raise a few pounds to do good deeds.

In any event the books were not sold. Or consigned to a cupboard. As far as I know, they are still lined up in a perfect Georgian bookshelf in one of those perfect Georgian rooms at No.1 Royal Crescent where the public can gaze at them to its heart's content for the modest price of admission. I certainly hope so, anyway, for the late James Lees-Milnes's sake. He was a sensitive soul, and a good man, and he did take things very seriously.

******

Another of my favourite "celebrated" customers was the journalist and author Miles Kington, who for more years than I can remember published a daily column in *The Independent* and was famous
for having coined the term "Franglais". The strain of creating a witty,
topical, 500-word article for a national newspaper six days a week
must surely have been intolerable, but Miles always seemed to bear
the burden with amazing nonchalance. Still, when the creative juices
weren't flowing, or he simply had too much else on his plate to get
those columns done, he knew he could always call on his friends to
help out. Sadly, Miles is no longer with us; he died in January 2008,
age 67, after a short struggle with pancreatic cancer. But I can still
remember him sitting cross-legged on the floor in his favourite corner
of the shop with a notepad on his knees, having announced that he
had to email in today's copy in three-hours' time, and would I mind
telling him anything amusing that had happened to me recently since
he had no idea what to write about. I would then gladly recount (or
even make up) anything entertaining or unusual that came to mind
while he took notes. After a few minutes he would put his pen away,
unwind from the lotus position, thank me and leave on his bicycle
back to his cottage in Limpley Stoke. Next morning, sure enough,
there would be my disjointed meanderings magically transformed
into a funny, telling, perfectly structured anecdote that *Independent*
readers would naturally assume had resulted from hours of concentrated wit and wisdom.

I particularly remember him coming into the shop one Friday
afternoon muttering, "Saturday column" to himself as he headed for
his corner.

"Cutting it a bit fine today, aren't we?" I said. It was nearly 3
p.m., just an hour short of submission time.

"Microscopic," he said, then explained that the time he should
have spent writing the Saturday column had been taken up delivering
a lunchtime talk on 'The Humourist's Flower Garden' to a group of
amateur horticultural enthusiasts from Yatton Kennel.

"Ghastly, stuffed matrons in pearl necklaces, and their pomp-
ous consorts wearing blue blazers with crests on the pockets. Crests,
for God sake! It was pure Graham Green . . ." he stopped talking

abruptly as we heard footsteps coming upstairs from the basement. After a moment an elderly, pompous-looking bald man wearing a blue blazer appeared on the top step carrying a £2 copy of *The Third Man* (I'm not making it up - it really was *The Third Man*.)

"One of my absolute favourites," he said, putting it on the desk with his two pounds. "Been wanting to re-read it for ages . . . "

Then as he turned to leave he caught sight of Miles sitting on the floor behind him. "Oh, Mr. Kington," he said. "You've just been speaking to our little group. Thank you so much. I hope it wasn't too great a bore for you. Wonderful about the herbaceous borders. Most amusing. Good bye."

Miles and I looked at one another as he left, looked outside until he'd disappeared down Margarets Buildings, looked back at one another again.

"Think he heard?" Miles said.

"Could have."

"Right, then," he said, standing up. "That's the Saturday column done. Buy you a coffee . . . ?"

In late November of 2008, Miles kindly accompanied me to a bi-annual get-together of the Omar Khayyam Club, a Victorian dining club, (of which I happened to be president that year) founded in the mid-nineteenth century by a group of like-minded English gentlemen for the purpose of celebrating the many accomplishments of the great Persian polymath/poet. (Also to enjoy, just as Omar would have wanted us to, a splendid meal, a lot of excellent wine, some terribly witty speeches, and a certain amount of schoolboy silliness.) As I'd suffered a stroke some months earlier that made travel on my own rather difficult, I'd arranged for Miles and me, plus another good friend, William Burman, to be taken to London by taxi and then brought back to Bath again when the revels had ended. Miles was wonderfully witty all the way there, and William and I were hoarse with laughter by the time we arrived. The dinner, as always, was held at the Savile, in that beautiful room with the bright blue ceiling painted with puffy white clouds. My speech, went rather well, I thought. My two guests were welcomed with great consideration. I did feel Miles was unusually quiet on the ride back, but we said goodbye

warmly as the taxi left to take him on home to Limpley Stoke. A few
weeks later, the sad news reached me that he had died.

Journalists can be a pain; especially the sardonic, self-important
variety. Miles was the opposite - he was a cure. One felt better just
being in his presence. Along with the *Independent* articles, the columns
he contributed to the *Oldie*, the many pieces he'd done for *Punch* in
his earlier days, and the books he'd written, Miles played double bass
in an amateur cabaret quartet called 'Instant Sunshine' that were in
constant demand simply because everyone liked the band members
so much. He filed his last *Independent* column only hours before he
died, I was told, and the book he'd written earlier on learning he was
dying, *How Shall I Tell The Dog*, appeared soon after.

******

The actress Jane Seymour OBE, is probably best remembered
for playing the lead in the American television series *Dr. Quinn, Medicine Woman*, and as the glamorous Solitaire in the 1973 Bond thriller,
Live and Let Die. She made her name in Hollywood but was in fact English (born in Hayes, Middlesex), and at the height of her fame, she
decided to buy herself an English country estate whence she and her
(fourth) husband, actor/director James Keach, could flee the mad-
ding crowd for a few weeks and commune in peace with some proper
ancient lawn. How she found the fourteenth century St. Catherine
Court in the St. Catherine valley north of Bath, I never knew. But
she did, and her weekend house parties, which often included lunch
at the Royal Crescent followed by a walk around Bath, meant that
she and her guests became frequent visitors to Bankes Books. They
were mostly film and television people, many of them American, but
to their credit I never once heard any of them use "cute" or "quaint"
in reference to the shop (though it was rather cute, in my opinion,
and I am most certainly quaint). Better still, they bought books. Some
very good ones, in fact - and quite a few, once it became clear that
the special discount offered by Mr. Bankes to Ms. Seymour would
also be extended to her friends. Thanks to the Medicine Woman, a
goodly number of finely bound sets of Shakespeare and Oscar Wilde

made their way to the United States by way of St. Catherine Court. I was most grateful to her for that, and I always tried to live up to her description of me as "that jolly man who finds such lovely books for everyone".

Speaking of lovely books, I recall one afternoon when she came in alone with her husband - in search of a gift, she said. On the table beside my desk, I'd placed on display an enormous, Victorian family Bible open at one of its very fine illustrations. While Ms. Seymour had gone downstairs searching, James Keach began studying the illustration, then carefully lifted the Bible in both hands, carried it to one of our easy chairs, settled it on his knees and began reading. Occasionally a distant voice could be heard calling, "Come and see this, darling!", but he seemed too absorbed to hear. Half an hour later, when Ms. Seymour returned from the basement bearing treasures, Keach stood up with the Bible in his arms, and said to her, "This is a great book! Why didn't anyone tell me about it? I'm buying this book and shipping it back to Beverly Hills." He turned to me. "I know the postage will cost me a fortune, but could you organise that for me, Mr. Bankes?"

A very pleasant moment, indeed - and perhaps as sincere an encomium as the Bible has ever received.

******

One evening in the autumn of 1990, Maryanne and I went to the Theatre Royal to see Joan Collins play Amanda in Private Lives, the role Gertrude Lawrence made famous in the 1930's. We didn't expect much from her, (celebrities, with rare exception, seem often to let themselves and their audiences down when they take on famous stage roles), but it was a play we both loved, and in fact Miss Collins surprised us by proving to be very good indeed.

The next morning, I went over to the shop early and sought out the copy of Noel Coward's collected works that I remembered had a frontispiece featuring a photograph of Coward and Lawrence facing one another across a breakfast table in a state of politely repressed fury. As I was examining the picture at my desk, a dark shadow fell across it. I looked up and saw a very large black straw hat shading a pair of enormous black sunglasses with the tip of a pert little nose, a red mouth and a small, perfectly-made chin peeking out beneath. Below those I saw a dazzling white blouse with frills in all the right places, and black jodhpurs fitting very tightly, also in all the right places. Clearly, I was in the presence of royalty, so I stood up at once and said:

"Good morning, Miss Collins. We did enjoy your very brilliant performance at the Theatre Royal last night. Thank you so much!"

In response to which she gave me a small, chilly smile, looked at her watch, wandered away among the bookshelves for a moment, then came back to the desk, scowled at me furiously and stormed out of the shop. (What I'd done wrong, I couldn't imagine, but because I am terribly sensitive to the nuances of artistic temperament, I decided it might not be the moment to run after her in the street, waving a £12 copy of Noel Coward's collected works shouting,

"Ten per cent discount if you'll sign our guest book, Miss Collins!")

I sighed, sat back down at my desk, and started going through the bills that had arrived that morning - when into the shop walked a tall, very good looking young man in an elegant white suit, who was also looking at his watch. I asked if I could help him find something. He said yes, then no, then he spotted the Noel Coward on my desk, still open to the frontispiece, and said,

"That!"

So I sold it to him, fairly certain that Miss Collins would not be returning that day - or, alas, ever. Whereupon she did return, still in storming mode.

"Where have you been?" she demanded of the young man in the white suit - who picked up his cue with perfect timing.

"Look what I got for you, my darling," and held forth the Coward, still open at the frontispiece.

"Oh, my darling," she burbled, "I've had booksellers all over London searching for this, and YOU found it for me!"

They walked out together, blissfully reunited, he with his arm around her slender waist, and she merrily swinging one of my famous bottle-green carrier bags.

Bankes Books one, puffed-up London bookdealers zero! I thought triumphantly to myself. Of course they'll never know who actually satisfied
Miss Collins, but never mind, that's show biz.

******

One fine Spring morning shortly after we'd opened Bankes
Books, a wonderful smile suddenly filled the doorway, followed immediately by a wheelchair. Seated in the chair was a handsome, grey-
haired woman in, I'd guess, her late forties, whom I'd seen occasionally in Bath but had never spoken to. She introduced herself as Liz
Pook, and shook hands with a firmness that surprised me. She then
asked, still smiling, to see my golf books, and when the young woman wheeling her chair had manoeuvred around to the section, she
managed, quite athletically, to take down from a high-ish shelf a thick
golfing encyclopaedia which she opened on her lap to the title page.
And then, to my horror, she began writing in the book with a fountain
pen. I stepped forward.

"I wonder . . . , " I said, hesitantly.

"It's all right. I'm only signing my name," she said, with that
same smile - accompanied this time by the happy twinkle of two
deep, deep blue eyes. She returned the encyclopaedia to its place in
the shelf, then asked me politely if I'd be kind enough to put aside any
books about lady golfers that came my way. "I'm keen to buy any title
I don't already have in my library," she explained, then said goodbye
and left the shop, still smiling, wheeled by her helper. After she'd gone,
I took down the book, of course, and looked at her signature. It wasn't
Pook. It was Chadwick - a name I recognised at once - Elizabeth
Chadwick, twice British Ladies Amateur Golf Champion, in 1966
and '67. (Which meant my golfing encyclopaedia was suddenly worth
twice what it had been two minutes before). Liz Pook was Chadwick's
married name I discovered when I flipped to her entry. I also discovered that in the 1967 final she'd been eight down with ten to play after
the turn, and that an extraordinary display of skill, courage and determination had carried her through to victory against overwhelming

odds. All the newspapers quite rightly praised her for her indomitable character as much as for her golfing prowess. A year later, though, an accident during surgery left her paralysed from the waist down. Since then, I assumed, she must have been slowly building up a comprehensive library of books about lady golfers. I knew there wouldn't be a great deal of literature on the subject, particularly from the years prior to the professional era. But having only just met her, I already had enormous admiration for her courage, and I was determined to find something really good for her. Eventually I did. It was an obscure collection of reprinted newspaper articles about the Scottish lady golfer, Dorothy Campbell, who was US amateur champion in 1909 and 1910, British ladies champion in 1909 and 1911, and then US champion again in 1924. She played under three different names (was married and divorced several times) and was renowned for her eccentric (and very effective) golf swing, for the accuracy of her short game, and for the sturdy, wide-brimmed straw hats she wore when competing.

The next time Ms. Pook came into the shop I earned another of those amazing smiles when I showed her what I'd found. She said she had known of the book, but had never been able to locate a copy, and I was then proud to be able to offer it to her as a gift. She was touched, and by way of thanks invited Maryanne and me to tea at her home near High Littleton to see what books she'd collected so far. A year or so later, Liz Pook moved away to, I think, Lancashire, where I gathered her children lived. I never saw her again after that, but I thought of her fondly whenever a lady golfer appeared on television, and I very much missed the visits of that brave, likeable, always beautifully smiling champion of my own favourite sport.

******

Joe Roberts, the Bath novelist and travel writer, began wandering into the shop soon after we'd opened, spending sometimes an hour looking through the bargains downstairs, and then another hour sprawled elegantly in the chair nearest my desk engaging me in heated conversation about his favourite subject: the pitfalls, injustices, and absurdities of a craft that seemed always to confound his ambition to be recognised as the good writer he was, and to make enough money doing it to support himself without having to prostitute his gifts. (Oh, we've all heard that one before! you'll be saying now. Another self-deluded genius, lamenting unjust treatment at the hands of a callous, unappreciative world.) Except that Joe's gifts were exceptional. And the world of publishing did seem to treat him with sometimes heart-breaking indifference.

Joe, who loved India deeply, published his first Indian travel book in January of 1995, a funny and very touching account of the time he had spent walking across Bangladesh, called *Three Quarters of a Footprint*. He was kind enough to invite us to the launch party, and I remember his mother saying to me proudly that she could now refer to Joe in all honesty as 'My son, the writer.'

"No, no," I corrected her, "you must say 'My son the *author*' - much more distinguished."

"Do you think he'll really be that one day?" she asked, sincerely.

"Yes, I do," I said. "Your son, the author, writes like an angel."

Some years later, Joe received the galley proofs of his next Indian book, *Abdul's Taxi to Kalighat*, about the months he'd spent living in Calcutta with his wife, Emma, and new baby son. He asked Maryanne and me to read the proofs, and was shocked to learn from us that they contained scores of typos and literals that his publisher's copy editor had either ignored or simply missed. Maryanne and I liked the book enormously, but even corrected, it did not achieve the success it deserved. Joe and I spent a lot of time in the shop discussing possible reasons why. We never came up with anything helpful, though - simply because the book Joe had written, (like *The Footprint* before it, which received excellent reviews but sold poorly) was perfectly fine as it was. Which, of course, left Joe right back where he'd started, stuck behind those mysterious pitfalls.

He wrote travel articles for *The Sunday Telegraph* and later for *The Times*, and Emma, who was his emotional and intellectual rock, worked as a PA and legal secretary, to keep the family afloat. But eventually, after their second son was born, Joe accepted a post in the creative writing faculty at Bath Spa University and is still there today.

At about that time, my good friend and neighbour, the editor George Kimball, worked briefly on the manuscript of the book Joe was then writing about Edward Lear's travels in Egypt; Joe, after all his set-backs was feeling uncertain about what he was doing, and Kimball's aim, as much as anything else, was to help him rediscover his confidence. In the end, though, he told me there was very little he could suggest beyond a bit of narrative tightening and the re-locating of one or two incidents, since what Joe had already written was quite simply his best work yet. "Maxwell Perkins might have had an idea or two," Kimball told me, "but I'm not altogether sure about that, and anyway he's dead."

In the end, the *Lear in Egypt* book was never published. On the other hand, writing students at Bath Spa University, can count themselves lucky to have such a gifted writer working with them.

******

And now, briefly, the story of a good deed. One morning in the winter of 1991, a tall, scholarly looking man with a ruddy complexion and clouds of white hair, walked into the shop and asked for the poetry section. I directed him to the basement, thinking, *why does this man look so familiar?* But it was only after he'd descended the stairs that I realised he was Robert Waller, BBC radio producer, ecological pioneer, outspoken anti-Thatcherite, and (in the 1930's) one of England's most promising young poets; one sufficiently gifted, in fact, to have earned the interest and support of T.S. Eliot. I calculated he would now be in his late 70's, which was why I hadn't immediately recognised him. And when he came back upstairs carrying three very good poetry collections (two Derek Mahons and a Seamus Heaney) the first thing he said was, "I've just walked here from Widcombe Crescent and now I'm going to walk back. Pretty good for 77, don't you think?"

"I do, indeed," I said.

"Nearly four miles round trip," he smiled, then extended his hand: "I'm Bob Waller, by the way."

I couldn't remember having ever read his poetry and I didn't want to admit I'd failed to recognise him when he came in, so I apologised and said, I'd thought it might be but wasn't sure.

He smiled again, a tiny bit sadly. "That does happen," he said, paid for his books, promised to come back soon, gave me a cheerful wave, and went out of the door with his poetry in a knapsack on his back.

Next morning he returned and bought two more poetry collections, both German translations this time. I offered him a coffee, which he readily accepted, and we sat at the desk for some time talking about modern poetry in general and his own in particular. (The previous evening Maryanne had unearthed a copy of his *The Two Natures* from our own books and as soon as I opened it I remembered that of course, I had read his work when it was published back in 1951, and that I had greatly admired it.) I told him I'd been looking through the collection the previous night and that his love poetry, remembered from 40 years ago, still struck me as particularly moving.

"Funny you should mention that," he said, opened his knapsack and passed me three A4 sheets of typing paper, with a single poem on each. I read through them while he sipped his coffee, then told him exactly what I thought about them. He picked up immediately on one phrase I used: that he seemed to be at heart a philosopher-poet. "That's exactly what T.S. Eliot said sixty years ago," he replied, again with that hint of sadness.

The next day when he came into the shop he showed me two more beautiful love poems and then took from his knapsack a manilla folder containing six long letters from Eliot offering him detailed criticism and encouragement (mostly the latter) following the publication of *The Two Natures*. The book, he told me, received fine reviews, but hardly sold at all; and that it was the last collection of his poetry ever to be published. He admitted that it hurt him - angered him, in fact - that publishers had ignored him for so long. Surely, he said, Eliot was a better judge than they?

He continued visiting the shop regularly over the next several months, sometimes to buy poetry but more often just to chat; and because he seemed to need to talk about himself, I learned a good deal about his life during that time. He'd been married three times, first to

Janet Truman, with whom he'd had two children. But their son Billy was tragically killed in a road accident in 1963, and Janet died of cancer seven years later in her early '50's. A brief second marriage, he said, was a rebound mistake, but he then married the actress Susan Dowdall, with whom he had 20 happy years until her death in 2000. He never stopped writing poetry, he said, despite his disappointments, but his professional life was devoted largely to his work at the BBC, where he produced programmes on poetry, philosophy and religion (Waller described himself as an "undogmatic Christian"), including the unforgettable debate between Bertrand Russell and Father Frederick Coplestone about the existence of God. After leaving the BBC he concentrated on his ecological and philosophical pursuits, served as editor of the *Soil Association Journal* from 1964 to 1970, and in 1973 published a polemical attack on industrial society (a book he confessed to being quite proud of) called *Be Human or Die*. All in all, he told me one day, he considered his life to have been a happy and fairly productive one - except for those unpublished poems.

Whereupon, enter the good deed - which was in fact Maryanne's idea. It was for her to edit the vast jumble of autobiographical material Bob had accumulated in cardboard boxes over the decades, turn it into a proper brief biography, combine it with a selection of his own best poetry, and have it published privately, with costs defrayed by selling the Eliot letters to the British Library. I put the plan to him the very next day - and six months later, in one of the State reception rooms of Bath's Pump Room, *The Pilgrimage of Eros, A Sequence of Poems and Sketches from an Autobiography*, by Robert Waller, was launched to heartfelt acclaim in a limited edition of 200 copies that had been printed and most elegantly bound in green cloth boards by one of England's finest private presses, Anthony Rowe, Ltd. Robert gave a very moving reading from the book, his health was toasted in champagne (several times, I recall), then all of his old friends, admirers and fellow rebels queued up to buy signed copies of the book. By the evening's end, nearly the entire edition had gone.

In 2005 Robert Waller died in a nursing home in Exeter at age 92. In his obituary, *The Guardian* described him as a cheerful prophet of doom and a delightful companion with a great sense of humour. I will certainly second the last two of these; of the first, I simply prefer to think of Bob Waller as a better realist.

Two or three copies of *The Pilgrimage* are still available online. The T.S. Eliot letters may now be seen in the British Library.

******

When giving directions to the shop, we were always proud to say "next door to the launderette." It was called 'The Spruce Goose' and in fact it supplied us with a number of customers over the years. Looking through the Visitors Book recently, I found that one Professor Charnley of William and Mary College in Maryland had written:

'A discussion about Tooke's Diversions of Purley, purchased from the bookshop next door while doing my laundry, proved both entertaining and surprising; certainly a great deal more diverting than watching my wet wash rotate. The Tooke was a bit more expensive than I could properly afford, but gave me a thoroughly enjoyable afternoon. For which I have to thank in equal measure Mr. Bankes, the bookshop's proprietor, and a splendidly smiley, West Country woman, named Julia who runs the launderette, and who urged me to look in next door for a good read to pass the time.'

Several other entries make similarly happy reference to the launderette. And while I can't remember a single time when Julia came into the shop to look for a book, I shall always be grateful for her loyalty to a fellow neighbourhood shop keeper.

******

William Burman, who accompanied Miles Kington and me to that meeting of the Omar Khayyam Club in London, came my way initially because running a shop six full days-a-week on my own seemed to tire me, and we decided a part-time helper might be a good idea. So for the first time Bankes Books did advertise - and our modest notice in *The Bath Chronicle* seeking a shop assistant provoked so many replies that I had to spend most of one night sorting through them - which of course left me even more tired the following morning.

We ruled out schoolgirls, all of whom insisted in their letters that they just loved books and then immediately wanted to know how much we were paying. Similarly the men and women with half-a-dozen degrees and expectations of vast salaries based on their dazzling qualifications (which often were dazzling) seemed in every case to stop short of understanding credit card machines. After a week of sifting we got down to six likely candidates, from which we finally chose Angela, who understood the importance of hoovering and dusting, needed the job but did not ask for an unrealistic salary, and most important of all, was not afraid of a credit card machine. Angela was a good choice. She stayed with us for over ten years, doing a day-and-a-half per week, and occasionally more when Maryanne and I had to be away. She left to get married, confessing to me that her new fiancé, like her three previous husbands, had met her through lonely hearts advertisements. She told Maryanne, (who had always been a pushover for confession stories), that her first two husbands had died early on in their married life, and the third, Angela confided a bit sheepishly, had curiously disappeared. Exactly the right background, we felt, for an assistant in a bookshop.

It was shortly after Angela left on her latest honeymoon that William appeared in Bankes Books. He introduced himself as having once run his own bookshop, and said he now had a roomful of books in a flat in Bath that he needed to get rid of. The flat was his wife's, but she would soon be giving it up to live in Australia (with another man, I assumed), so the books needed to be cleared out pretty quickly. I went round to see them that evening, and indeed there were some quite interesting titles - including an early edition of Gilbert White's *Natural History of Selborne* - but far more interesting than the books, was William's unexpected suggestion that since Angela was leaving my employ (he'd known her for years, it turned out), perhaps he might take her place in the shop one or two days a week. I said yes immediately. Maryanne said yes as soon as I told her. And the very next day William became my new shop assistant.

William Burman, then in his early 60's, was by vocation an

Anglican clergyman of the peripatetic kind. Tall, slender, extremely good-looking with white wavy hair, blue eyes, and a deep, reso-
nant voice, he was at the time I engaged him, the priest in charge
of the chapel of ease at Holloway in Bath. He actually belonged in
a Barchester novel dispensing wry wisdom to the congregation with
the distaff side of his flock adoring him from the pews. Educated and
effortlessly charming, he proved to be a valuable addition to the shop
and in time became an excellent friend, as well. He was also a sort
of magnet for women customers. Within weeks of my hiring him,
their numbers seemed to double on the days when he was on duty,
and when word got round that he was divorced (or about to be), their
numbers more or less doubled again. Marvellous for business, of
course, but at times a rather complicating issue for William, who was,
unlike your classical Don Juan, as much of a pushover for the charms
of the adoring ladies as they were for his. Scrapes involving jealous
husbands or narrow-minded boyfriends must surely have blown up
from time to time, but I never saw or heard evidence of one in the
shop, and I suspect that William had long since developed strategies
for smoothing these over with the sort of charming diplomacy that
would have made Mr. Trollope nod most approvingly.

After he'd been at the shop for several years, William asked unexpectedly if he could take some holiday time starting on such-and-such
a date and ending about two weeks later. The starting date was un-
changeable, he said, and I explained that this happened to clash with
arrangements of my own. But when he made clear the circumstances, I told him I'd be happy to change my plans to accommodate his. It
seems William had been asked to act as locum for a clergyman friend
who was vicar of the English Church in Stresa, on the shores of Lago
Maggiore. For William it would be two weeks of wholly undemand-
ing duties in one of the most beautiful, romantic, matron-rich holiday
resorts in the world. It would have been worth closing the shop for
those two weeks rather than deny William the chance to take advan-
tage of such an irresistible opportunity.

And on his return from Paradise, he admitted (without elaborat-
ing) that his two weeks had been what he called 'a success' - so much
so, indeed, that his friend had asked him to take on the same arduous

task the following year - and the next. I kept wanting to ask William
if I could tag along one year as altar boy or incense swinger or something else minorly ecclesiastical - but I'm not as young as I was, and
decided against it.

******

Among my much-loved cavalcade of customers, was David Wearson, a tall, faintly languid, less than rigorously-minded middle-aged
gentleman, always impeccably dressed and groomed when he came
into the shop, whom Maryanne and I came gradually to think of as
"The Unrequited Lover."

On his first visit to the shop he was wearing a white linen suit and
he politely removed his Panama hat before asking me if I knew of any
good books to give a girl. It emerged that he was obliged to go to La-
gos for six months because of his dealings in the oil business, and he
wanted to give his Scottish girlfriend . . . "Well, you know, something
just right, to say, goodbye."

"A book of poetry might be the right thing," I suggested, at which
his brows knitted.

"I'm not much of a one for poetry, I'm afraid."

I took a gamble: "'My love is like a red, red Rose,'" I recited, and
his brows immediately cleared. "It's by Robert Burns," I said. The
brows knitted again. "The great Scottish poet," I said. "Your girlfriend might appreciate that."

In the shelf behind my desk, I had a nicely bound *Poems of Robert
Burns* which I pulled out and handed to him.

"This looks nice," he said, holding it as one might hold a live
hand grenade. "Um, where will I find that poem you just said about
a rose?"

I told him the page, he read through the poem twice with obvious
appreciation. Then, "Do you think it would be all right to send her
this with some red roses?"

To which I replied firmly: "Any girl would be delighted." Deal
done. He paid in cash, thanked me profusely and left, shoulders
squared, to find a flower shop.

I honestly didn't expect to see the man again. But six months later, quite possibly to the day, there he was, standing before my desk in his white tropicals and Panama hat.

"Would you have any books suitable for a sort of 'Hallo again' present? And, Mr. Bankes, before I forget, she did like that Burns thing with the roses."

"In that case," I said (God knows why but I was actually beginning to like this man), "What about the collection, *English Love Songs?*"

Again the knitted brow: "Don't you think that might be coming on a bit strong?"

Possibly, I thought, if Victoria were still on the throne. So instead of the love songs, I got down a full calf, Bowdlerised edition of *Romeo and Juliet*. He was delighted to have heard of those two, but had to ask about this "Bowdle-whatsit business - it isn't rude, or anything, is it?" So instead of giving him a Bowdlerised explanation, I searched out volume one of Dr. Bowdler's notorious 10-volume Shakespeare, first published in 1818, and read out the pertinent line from the introduction: ". . . in which nothing is added to the original text; but those words and expressions are omitted which cannot with propriety be read aloud in a family." And again, the brow cleared miraculously and off he went to reacquaint himself with his lady love.

He returned to the shop several times subsequently to contribute to the swelling of his beloved's library - once at Christmas, again in June (her birthday), and again in autumn for a bonfire night treat. As the book-buying proliferated, however, I began to have the uneasy feeling that Mr. Wearson was not first in line, or even fifth or sixth, in the affections of the bonnie maiden from Scotland. And sure enough, early that December, he came into the shop and asked morosely if I had a good book to say goodbye with.

"Back to Africa?" I asked him.

He nodded. I didn't ask if it was oil interests again, or shooting lions. It was obviously unrequited love, poor man, and I couldn't ask about that. I thought first of *A Room with a View* as a fitting valedictory, with particular reference to Lucy Honeychurch's fiancé, Cecil. But I changed my mind and suggested instead: "I could not love thee dear so much/ Loved I not honour more . . ."

He knitted for a moment, then un-knitted, thanked me, said that would do very well indeed, and left, swinging his green carrier bag.

He has not been back. For all I know, he lives now in a bachelor flat in Lewes or Fowey. I prefer, though, to imagine him still in Africa, wearing his white suit and a pith helmet, accompanied by half-a-dozen local girls all vying desperately for his attention.

******

Mr. Brown had a great appreciation for the style and quality of a once-famous series of illustrated travel guides published by A & C Black at the turn of last century. What was unique about these guides, and a thoroughly splendid idea, was that the illustrations were produced first and the text afterwards. Thus, the publishers would commission an artist of repute to visit a well-known tourist destination - Naples, for example, or the Riviera, and then hire a travel journalist of equal repute to write appropriate text to elaborate upon the views. Blacks invested heavily in this project, maintaining the highest possible standards by refusing to skimp on paper quality, colour reproduction, page design, binding and indeed artist's and writer's fees.

It was a risky undertaking, but the risk was more than amply rewarded, as the announcement of each new volume in the series generated greater and greater advanced sales among a growing army of enthusiasts. Its volumes have become collectors' items, and Mr. Brown was one of the keenest of those collectors. Whenever a copy of one came my way I would contact him immediately. He would only buy fine copies, quite rightly, too, though his standards cost me a number of sales. But he always paid well and I learned to forgive him for always accompanying a purchase with, "Now you're quite sure this is a good investment?"

The market for these books was actually strongest in the 1970's and 1980's, but in the '90's and early 2000's when Mr. Brown was doing his most serious collecting, the market was still very good. Then one of those disasters that only dedicated book collectors understand befell Brown's travel guides. His son, Chippie Brown, came into the shop one morning to say that his parents had moved to a smaller house recently, and that, "My father says the removals people have mucked up the A & C Blacks. The insurance company says they're all there, so they see no grounds for a claim. Can you do something, Mr. Bankes? My father was sure you could."

I had rather less faith than Mr. Brown in my ability to do something, but I went round to have a look at the books. And once I'd seen the state they were in, I went straight home and wrote the following letter to Mr. Brown's insurers:

> *Dear Sir,*
>
> *When I saw the state of Mr. Brown's A & C Black collection, I was most distressed. He had rightly collected only books of high quality in 'Very Good' condition (only 'Mint' ranks higher in auction valuation). Mr. Brown bought many of these books from me, and was always meticulous in checking boards, spine, pages and general condition before purchasing. The books I have just examined appear to have been savagely rammed into tea chests, scuffing or ripping the boards of nearly every volume. It is a very sad sight. This series of books is valued for its quality and condition, NOT for its quantity! The fact that all of the books were delivered to Mr. Brown is of little consequence. What is of consequence, is the deplorable condition in which they reached him. Before this assault by vandals, the collection was worth at auction £2800 - £3300. Today it is worth £150 - £250. I should be happy to discuss this sad matter further if you wish.*

Chippie told me later that his father's insurers had finally come up with £3000 for the damaged books, and asked if I wanted to buy the Rottweiler-ed remains. I declined politely, but Chippie very decently remembered that I charged a 10% valuation fee and sent me a cheque for £300. (If anyone reading this is in need of assistance with insurance companies, I am also prepared to write trenchant letters about mismanaged weddings, divorces, bungled travel plans, bar mitzvahs, etc. . . .)

Mrs. Margerison lived in Marlborough Buildings, that very tall

Georgian terrace just the far side of the Royal Crescent. She was an occasional rather than a regular customer, and I remember she came into the shop to see me one morning dressed in a most elegant dark blue suit with white at the neck and cuffs, and wearing a very ladylike hat with a net veil sprinkled with those curious black blobs that look disconcertingly like squashed gnats. She said good morning in her usual polite way, but then seemed a bit uncertain as she made her way across to the shelves of leather-bound books. After standing there for several minutes, looking steadily more uncertain, she returned to the desk and said, "My husband has never been in so you won't know him, but he is, in fact, Sir Cyril Margerison - and I am actually Lady Margerison, you see, though I don't use it in Bath."

Except to booksellers, I thought.

"It is our Silver wedding anniversary tomorrow, and Cyril hinted that he'd quite like a first edition of *Dombey and Son*."

I started to say I could certainly supply her with such an article, but she went straight on:

"I am confused, however, about 'issue points'. They seemed terribly important to Cyril, whatever they may be, and he did try to explain, but I couldn't seem to catch on and I could feel we were heading toward the quicksand, metaphorically speaking, so just before I sank into the slime or a terrible row broke out, he said, 'Oh, do go and ask your nice Mr. Bankes to explain so we can save our marriage, for God's sake', and went off to bed with a whiskey."

She stopped short and looked at me through her veil - beseechingly, I assumed - though the squashed gnats made accurate interpretation a bit tricky.

"For the sake of your marriage, Lady Margerison," I said gallantly, went to the Dickens shelves, took down our first edition *Dombey*, and carried it back to the desk. "Now. 'Issue points', also called 'points of interest', are simply mistakes made during the printing of the first edition of any book. If they are caught before distribution begins, they may be corrected, the book reprinted, and what we call a slightly later issue of the first edition will appear for sale. Both versions are, properly speaking, first editions. But the earlier version, the printing that contains the uncorrected mistakes, will be of greater value, generally speaking, than the corrected version; like a postage stamp printed upside-down, or with the Queen looking in the wrong direction. You can still read the book with its mistakes, and you can still post a letter with your backward Queen, but in both instances the auction value of the mistaken issue will be higher - in some cases, very much higher. Okay so far?"

She nodded, looking greatly relieved (I think, anyway).

"Everything gets a bit trickier with Dickens, however," I continued. "If you'll open the *Dombey* to the front free paste-down page, you'll see I've written at the top in pencil, 'First edition in book form' and the date 1848. But the story was actually first published in serial form between October 1846 and April 1848 in the magazine *Household Words* - 20 instalments printed in 18 numbers of the magazine - two at the beginning, two at the end. Now, many people kept all the numbers and had them bound into book form after the last instalment appeared. Those that still exist are considered first editions as well. There are also slightly earlier first editions than the first edition in book form that you are holding, since the last instalment in the magazine was published a few months before the book. But that is only of interest to the collectors we call 'anoraks'. Your husband, I'm guessing is not one of those."

"He wouldn't be caught dead in an anorak," she said, and laughed brightly behind her veil.

"Now," I said, "if you will turn forward three pages to the frontispiece, Lady Margerison, you will see something that I guarantee will preserve your marriage 'til the end of time - or at least until your husband stops worrying about issue points."

She did as I asked, looked, looked some more, looked up at me. "All I see is the painting of an old naval officer with a hook for one hand."

"That is Captain Cuttle," I said.

She went on looking at me.

"Painted by the renowned Victorian illustrator Hablot Knight Browne. A perfect rendition of the Captain as Dickens describes him in the text - except for one thing."

"What thing?"

"Dickens introduces us to Captain Cuttle as 'an old seafaring man who lost his right arm in some hostilities and wears a hook in its place' . . ." I paused and nodded again at the illustration. She looked back at it for several seconds, then:

"Oh, my goodness, it's on the wrong hand - Cyril will love it!"

"My favourite issue point in all of literature," I said. "Corrected, of course, by the deeply embarrassed artist before the second edition appeared, but there are still a few of the first firsts around. And that one is yours, if you're happy with it."

"I am delighted with it!" said Lady Margerison.

"Good. I'll just put it in a carrier bag for you."

******

Mr. Ballantyne was a regular visitor who most kindly explained in a soft Welsh accent that he stopped in so frequently because Bankes Books was on his way home. He always dressed in black, with a bit of white shirt showing at the collar which made me surmise at first that he might be a clergyman doing something half incognito (whatever that might be), then later that he might be a soft-spoken Welshman who merely liked to pretend he was a clergyman, or who had been a clergyman but had lapsed (this, because he could not resist ogling pretty girls who walked past in Margarets Buildings, something a lapsed clergyman might well do - especially if pretty girls were the cause of his lapsed-ness). He never bought books, but had a favourite topic of conversation he liked to draw me into - The Maccabees.

For example: "Are the Maccabees totally wrong," he would ask as he walked in the door, "or just a little bit wrong?" Then seeing I had no idea what he was talking about today, he would sit down at the desk and patiently explain about the Maccabees' position on the difference between good and evil so that I could join in the discussion. He also liked, as a change of pace, to discuss the Latin or Greek he found worked into the designs of bookplates in the books he never bought.

Now, you can be sure that the most embarrassing moments in any shop will inevitably occur when it's full of people. And so it was, late one Saturday morning, when Ballantyne burst into a crowd of customers, drunkenly waving his arms about, and demanding at the top of his voice to see my "Early Christshun Heretic Sheckshun!"

Everyone in the shop froze and became immediately absorbed in whatever book he or she was looking at, but all ears were pricked, and there was that atmosphere of mass frisson that instantly permeates moments like this. I didn't think Ballantyne was dangerous - if I had I wouldn't have done what I did next. I did think, however, that he might cause a lot of trouble if I didn't act fast, so I got up from my desk, crossed to the door, placed my considerable bulk, arms spread wide, between Mr. Ballantyne and my customers, and started an ushering back outside manoeuvre, like a sheep herder shoo-ing a troublesome ram away from the frightened ewes. What on earth I would have done if Ballantyne had flung himself into my apparently welcoming embrace, I can't imagine. But I kept edging him back toward the door, all the while murmuring soothing words about the 'Christshun Heretics' being just along here. When I'd got him back outside I pointed him up Margarets Buildings. He seemed perfectly happy to keep walking - weaving, actually - in that direction, and my main concern now was that he might get home safely.

Back in the shop, I noticed the atmosphere had changed abruptly. No one said anything, but after a moment my customers gave me a very English, embarrassed round of applause. Then still without a word, the applause stopped and they all went back to studying their books.

I noticed later, though, that the shop's takings for that Saturday morning were considerably greater than usual.

******

Earlier that same morning, our good friend and next door neighbour in Brock Street, George Kimball, came into the shop with the jumbo cryptic crossword from the *Saturday Times*. As there were no customers in as yet, we went to work on it at once at my desk, and had just completed the top left corner when Maryanne appeared to say the wheelbarrow had been delivered from Homebase.

"It's in a vast cardboard box with instructions for assembly."

"Assembly? But the one in the shop . . . " I began, when two customers, the Borden-Smith's came in, and the day had begun.

"Would you like me to have a go?" George offered, standing up from the desk.

"Would you mind?" Maryanne asked.

"I'd be delighted," he said, and out they went.

George was an expatriate Californian with a fine white walrus moustache, who might have been mistaken for Mark Twain had his shape been more like Mr. Clemens's and less like mine. He'd worked in Hollywood as a young man, published some very fine short stories, lived in the South of France for twelve years where he met his English wife, the beautiful Rosalind, and since returning with her to England - first London, then Bath - had been a film critic and book reviewer, written a guide book to the London theatre, co-authored guides to the food and wine of several European countries (his specialty in these being comprehensive glossaries that any English-speaker could pronounce like a native), and now worked mainly as a free-lance editor for publishers and private clients. He was, by all accounts, a very good writer indeed. But in my view his real gifts were as a solver of puzzles, an assembler of flat-packed wheel-barrows, and greatest of all, as a barbecue-ist.

Kimball's prowess with cryptic puzzles, while certainly impressive, was as nothing to his annual triumphs with the notorious Christmas quiz compiled each holiday season by the Reverend Benchly, of West Kington. Each year, our mutual friend, Rachel Huxley, received in the post from a clerical Huxley whose name I have forgotten, a copy of Reverend Benchly's fiendish, 100-question brain-teaser. Merely to be included in the competition was an honour, but it was Rachel's ambition, nothing short of obsessive, to answer all 100 questions correctly and win the first prize - a rather stingy food hamper and a bottle of Bollinger, if I remember. Though what she really sought, of course, was the glory. Deadline for submission was 15th December, and somewhere around the 1st Rachel would appear in the shop with her answers all filled in except for about a dozen which she simply couldn't get. Would George and I have a go? As a reward for our help she promised to submit her entry as Rachel Huxley and Friends. Neither George nor I gave a damn about the prize or the glory, but the challenge of a dozen really tough quiz questions? Red rag! To our chagrin, we never did get all the missing answers, but we usually whittled Rachel's dozen down to one or two - and it was invariably the triple-level pun about some utterly obscure film and the question requiring the lateral thinking skills of a lunatic that George invariably got. Rachel's submission, 98-out-of-100 - once even 99 - never took the prize, though. Each year, in fact, the winner was the same elderly woman from the depths of Wiltshire who always scored 100-out-of-100. (George was convinced this woman was a fiction and that the actual winner was a 19-year-old girl from the parish with a key to the vicarage's back door - but then Americans will think that way.)

Despite our annual shortcomings, Rachel never lost faith in us as potential winners, and we played the roles of 'And Friends' for many, many years.

Kimball's second great skill, wheel barrow assembly, can be summed up in one sentence: I couldn't have done it better, myself. (Or maybe not at all!)

As for cooking out of doors over open flame, suffice it to say for now, that when a man is born and raised in California, as Kimball was, then if he is anything less than a world-class barbecue-ist, he will be judged a traitor to his pioneer heritage and may be cast into the Nevada desert for an eon by the secret board of elders who determine such punishments. Kimball was not such a traitor; for his sausages were in truth sublime. And so, indeed, were his chops!

******

Among our neighbours in Margarets Buildings were a very good Lebanese restaurant run by Mr. Haddad, a rather dashing, slightly Byronic character from Beirut, and a very good delicatessen run by Michael Robinson, a handsome, terribly good-natured, Hugh Grant-ish looking public school boy from Hampshire who eventually opened a gastro-pub in Berkshire and became, for a time, a popular TV chef.

Further along the street was the Vendange, a bar-restaurant known mainly for its congeniality rather than the quality of its food, which was run, as I've already mentioned, by a retired girls' public school headmistress, called Shaw; she poured a very generous drink and was the soul of congeniality, herself, as well as the potential source of any and all local gossip one might require. Between these three, one could find nourishment for all the parts without ever having to walk more than a few dozen paces from the door of the book shop. If one needed antiques of a superior sort, there was Kit Alderson down at the Brock Street end of the Buildings. And if one needed amazingly quirky, useless things - a stuffed moose-head for example, or a Sousaphone, or a selection of shell casings from the Boer War - there was Brian Kraik Antiques across from the Vendange. (Mr. Kraik, alas now gone, was an upper-class anarchist who actually looked a bit like Lenin. Given the least encouragement, he would engage one in the street, in rambling political argument about almost anything, employing language so arcane and vehement that it was impossible to follow what he was saying, or even to grasp who or which injustice he was being furious about today.)

Back along the street and across from us, was Kraik's opposite, (antidote might be more accurate), the gentle, always softly spoken Andrew, who sold alternative and new age books, and who once asked me if I would be willing to drive to a village in Dorset where his aunt had recently died leaving him a house and its contents, including quite a large library.

"Matilda's books may be of no interest to you, of course," he said, almost apologetically, "so do make an offer on any of the porcelain if you so wish."

Full of high hopes, Maryanne and I set off the following Sunday, got lost several times among the lanes and hedges of Dorset, but found the place eventually - more importantly, found the key where Andrew said it would be - and flung ourselves cheerfully at the books. There were no 'sleepers', unfortunately, but we did find some good shop stock which we earmarked for purchase, and then turned our attention to the porcelain. Some of this was lovely, and Maryanne was able to price it accurately enough for us to be able to present Andrew with a substantial cheque on our return - an unexpected windfall, he said, which he described as "highly gratifying."

Andrew became a good friend over the years and was always happy to demystify arcana-like lay lines and druidic dances for me whenever I found myself in possession of books on subjects of that sort. At school he had once come off his bicycle going down a steep hill, and had smashed a number of bones in his arms and hands which could never be fully repaired. I admired the way he coped with this, knowing myself how difficult books are to handle even when one has the full use of one's hands.

I was always happy to send people looking for books on alternative medicine or primitive religions across the street to him. And when he sold the shop eventually and moved to South Africa, I found I missed our regular chats over coffee at Michael's deli or the Vendange more than I would have imagined.

*****

In a sort of perverse compensation for Andrew's departure, however, there was Patrick. More giant medicine ball than mortal man, with cropped grey hair, an apoplectically red face, and a perpetual stubble beard (long before stubble was trendy), he favoured yellow waistcoats, drove a huge old Jaguar Saloon, and was, as one of his erstwhile associates once described him, "Your typical Brighton antiques hustler." (Generosity of spirit forbids me going too deeply into that subject, and nothing was ever proven, of course; but suffice it to say, he was not a high end dealer like Kit Alderson, nor a dealer in eccentric curiosities like Brian Kraik, but something in-between whose associations with the back ends of lorries might not be entirely irrelevant.)

Patrick had taken the shop next to the Vendange only weeks after Andrew departed. He introduced himself to us the day he arrived and immediately began extolling his latest selling triumph - something about a pine chest he'd had 'restored' (for which read, 'doctored') to its Georgian origins and turned over at a ridiculous profit. No money-making scheme, it appeared, could fly anywhere near

Patrick without him making a grab at it. And very soon Maryanne and I began thinking enviously of how quickly his stock seemed to turn over. Suites of furniture, dining tables and chairs, huge wardrobes would appear in Margarets Buildings on a Monday morning and be gone 72 hours later. Like a magician's trick. When I mentioned this to Kit, he gave me a wry look and then explained that Patrick, whom he'd known for years (but steadfastly refused to speak to), had another shop in Brighton. "He's probably moving the pieces down there. And bringing other pieces from there up here."

"Why would he do that?" I asked him.

He looked at me thoughtfully. "I think I'll leave you to figure that out, Anthony."

Outside his shop each morning, Patrick placed a department store mannequin dressed as a guardsman wearing a busby. This attracted a lot of attention from tourists, especially Americans - which is why he put it there - but he confessed to me one day that he'd learned from an associate that every busby was marked inside with its owner's ID number, and that every time anyone inspected the hat too closely he became fearful that the MP's would arrive and march him off to Caterham barracks where he'd be left to rot under martial law. It was a ridiculous idea, and I don't think Patrick believed a word of it. But it was the sort of story he liked to tell - to make himself look important, I imagine, or to enlist sympathy for his perilous existence - and that always made me feel a little sad for him. Inside the bulk and the bluster and the bragging, was a frightened little man who'd been faking his own importance for so long he probably didn't know it was faking anymore. He probably actually believed people were impressed with him because he drove a Jaguar. And that, as I said to Maryanne, really was sad.

So I was friendly to him, despite not liking who he was much, but I'm afraid I let him down rather badly on one occasion. It began when he came into the shop near closing time one summer afternoon and whispered (any ordinary message was always a state secret, with Patrick), that he'd just been buying furniture from a Miss Cobbs at a rather nice house near Tetbury. "Hunting family, father's just died, daughter's decided to leave the country, selling up everything."

He'd been asked his advice about who might buy all the hunting books in her father's bedroom and in the attic.

"Of course I suggested you," Patrick said, and then added that Miss Cobbs would not be there, but would appreciate my visiting the house that same evening as she was anxious to clear things up as quickly as possible.

I found my way to the house after the usual number of missed turns in the dark. It was a large, stockbroker Tudor with five bedrooms - not quite 'hunting family' standard, but that's Patrick. A neighbour let me in, and I soon found the bedroom that was clearly the old man's. By the bed, half-opened as if someone had been reading it aloud to the dying man and had laid it down so as not to lose the place, was my favourite book, *Mr. Sponge's Sporting Tour*, and my heart went out to the family at once. There were several other Surtees stories on the shelf beside the bed, plus four Snaffles books, a Bible and a prayer book. The condition of these were what booksellers describe to potential buyers as 'a trifle dusty', and when buying to resell as 'scuffed and grubby'. I found no books in the reception rooms downstairs, but a peek in the kitchen showed a little row of three eighteenth century cookery books and two manuscript books of 'receipts' from the late sixteenth century. All were comparatively clean, something unusual for books kept and used in a kitchen. Even so these five, plus the books I'd seen in the bedroom, hardly justified the long drive from Bath to Tetbury and back. Perhaps the books Patrick said were in the attic would make the trip worthwhile.

As it turned out, there was no attic, but eventually I found a ladder leading to a loft above one of the bedrooms, and I climbed it wondering who would ever find me if I fell and broke my leg in this empty house. I pushed open the trap, crawled into the loft, found the chain that switched on a bare bulb in a bright red shade, and head carefully bowed so I didn't crack it on the low beams, I began going through the five large piles of books I found there, roughly half of them hunting books, as promised. Some were water damaged; others were still in saleable condition. Parliament had only recently enacted the fox hunting ban, so I feared the hunting books might not sell as well as I would have liked, but I was still happy enough to write Miss

Cobbs a cheque for £700 and give it to the neighbour who had let me into the house.

The next day, Patrick came around early, anxious to know how much I had spent, and after a couple of evasions like, "A good deal," and "More than I should have," I realised he wasn't going to drop it and told him what I'd given Miss Cobbs. I also realised why he was so insistent on knowing (subtlety was not one of Patrick's greater gifts). He was waiting for me to offer him a finder's fee. As I'd no intention of doing that, and he showed no sign of going away, I finally said I had a lot of work to do cleaning up the books I'd driven 80 miles round trip last night to buy for too much money, and he reluctantly left - sulking.

I told Maryanne the story after supper that evening and she produced from one of her secret hoards of treasures, the scarlet tunic her grandfather had worn at official get-togethers as Lord Lieutenant of Lancashire. "Give him this to tart up his guardsman," she said. "Quite wrong with a busby, of course, but he won't know that and neither will the tourists."

Patrick seemed quite pleased with the tunic next morning, especially when he'd carried it outside, draped it over the guardsman's shoulders and seen how splendid it looked. But I could see he was still sulking; that finder's fee would have been 10% of £700, and I suppose he could have used it. On the other hand, I also supposed he would sell the tunic at the earliest opportunity for a good deal more than £70, and then make up some implausible story about thieves to explain to us why it had suddenly disappeared.

Such a lovable rogue, was Patrick. There was talk in the Buildings of throwing him a farewell party when he announced he would be leaving Bath soon. (Actually he left rather more suddenly than 'soon', as it turned out.) What a nice idea, everyone said. But strangely enough, he was gone before the party ever got organised.

CHAPTER FIVE: THIEVES

"Gorrit from a fren, dint I?"

Thieves represent the dark side of a bookseller's life, not only because an expensive book one may have driven miles to acquire and spent hours collating and preparing for sale suddenly disappears, but because the *idea* of some innocent looking soul among one's customers pretending sedately to browse the shelves while secretly waiting for an opportunity to steal, leaves a sad taste of gall in the mouth.

Nor is the Romance of Thievery a notion I subscribe to. I remember colleagues in the Wednesday market telling me with awe about a man in a long overcoat who once stole - in a single visit - a complete 12-volume encyclopaedia from the very basement sale room where I later had my stall. I never quite believed that story, but the relish with which it was told made me think of the excitement aroused in small children by the likes of *Robin Hood and The Thief of Baghdad*. It also made me recall, to my acute embarrassment, how in Woolworth's one day, when I was nine years old, I had stood looking longingly at a cheap little gold-coloured make-up compact, that seemed suddenly to glide into my hand and thence into my pocket. When I got home, I handed it proudly to my mother, who with astonishing powers of divination seemed to know at once that it had come from Woolworths - and that it had not been paid for. She telephoned the manager, and the next day I found myself standing before his desk, eyes downcast, mumbling a confession (which included, "I only wanted to give Mummy something nice!"), then handing over the compact along with a pathetic little bundle of my week's pocket money, and finally being subjected to what used to be called 'a wigging' by the manager, whose theme was the swift downhill path from petty pilfering to Perdition. On the bus ride home my mother, though cross, admitted it was rather sweet that I'd stolen something for her, and not even for her birthday. The lesson was learnt, though - I never stole again.

Along with books, the theft of cash is a shopkeeper's constant worry. I didn't have a proper cash till - my desk was too small - so my top middle drawer became the till. I protected this by removing knobs from the front, and opening it by reaching under the desk and wiggling it out with my finger-tips. Whether cash-thieves knew I had done this and decided it was too awkward to get into quickly, or decided there wasn't enough in it to bother with, we never lost any cash to thieves in twenty years. We never had a cheque bounce, either, or a stolen credit card presented.

We did have book thieves, though; enough to make a difference to the weekly balance sheet. And like nearly all shop keepers, we never found a really effective way to thwart the determined ones. The downstairs room was usually their hunting ground of choice, and if one or two descended, especially those wearing loose jackets, stayed for several minutes, then returned saying they couldn't find what they were looking for, I would sometimes try the ploy of standing by the front door and asking pointedly if there were anything else I could help them find. But as citizen's body-search is against the law, and self-preservation doth make cowards of us all, there was little I could do if they said, "No - just browsing today," except to hold the door open for them, wish them bon voyage, then go downstairs and try to determine what, if anything, was missing. There was a period in the early 90's when Stevie Smith and Wilfred Owen were de rigueur among my downstairs book thieves - and I sometimes wondered if

Stevie and Wilfred wouldn't have felt rather proud to be so honoured by the light-fingered of Bath. We did have our CCTV cameras of course, courtesy of the insurance company, and every so often I would be invited down to the Police station to compare my daily tapes with their latest mug shots of shop lifters. The result over the years was exactly what I'd suspected it would be - I never made a single match.

******

Thieves, I learned, appear in many guises, and rather like those who come in the night, always unexpected ones. A well-known and distinguished citizen of this city, who I will refer to simply as Mr. A, used to come into the shop perhaps twice a month and head straight for the shelf reserved for early editions of books by and about John Milton, probably the most admired of all English poets save Shakespeare, and almost certainly the least read. Mr. A would regularly stand before the Milton shelf looking carefully at one book and then another for as long as half an hour. The shelf was directly opposite my desk, only ten feet away, so I had a clear view of his back; and when he'd finished perusing, we would often spend several enjoyable minutes chatting about the special character and peculiarities of early Milton editions. This distinguished gentleman never bought a book from me. But after he'd been paying his regular visits for several months it became clear to me that my stock of early Miltons was steadily diminishing without a corresponding increase in my bank balance. Obviously, someone was stealing early Miltons, and as Mr. A was the only one of my customers who regularly visited those shelves, I determined to watch him more closely next time he came in. This I duly did during three more visits - and detected exactly nothing untoward. So at the end of his fourth visit, having nothing to lose, I called across to him as he was going out of the door, "Would you like to pay for that now, Mr. A, or on your next visit?"

"Oh, now would be fine," he said, not losing a beat. "Usual discount?"

As I handed him his change, I almost asked him about the other Miltons that had gone missing, but I didn't have the nerve.

Several months later I heard that Mr. A had died. A month or so after that, a pleasant looking woman of patrician background came into the shop, followed by a young man carrying a box of books. She introduced herself as Mrs. A, and said her husband had left a note amongst his papers saying these books were to come to me. "He left the rest of his lovely library to our son, but he insisted these were to be returned to you with thanks for having so generously lent them to him for his researches."

Sure enough, in the box were all of my "stolen" early Miltons - plus two more Miltons (with all pencil marks carefully erased). How he got my books out of the shop without my noticing, I will never know. But I still remember Mr. A, the Milton thief, for the graceful way he found of paying his debt to bookselling society with the gift of two extra books, perhaps similarly acquired, by a poet we both admired.

******

The Antiquarian Booksellers' Association (ABA) and the Provincial Booksellers' Fairs Association (PBFA), joined forces some years ago to develop an effective anti-theft strategy designed to put every member of either society on the look-out for the appearance of stolen books. Each member is assigned the names, email and telephone numbers of two other designated members. When any member discovers a book has gone missing, he can immediately advise his two names, who in turn will each advise their two names, and within hours the entire membership will have been alerted to keep an eye out for the stolen property described.

The system works equally effectively as a means of spreading the descriptions of the thieves, themselves; most of whom, having successfully stolen a book worth, say, £100 from one dealer, will give themselves away by trying quickly to unload it on another dealer for a mere £10 or even £5. I had such an experience myself less than a year after we opened, when a scruffy young man displaying bags of nerve, offered to sell me for £12, a first edition Middlemarch that was actually marked in pencil on the flyleaf at £150. Either this scruff was seriously innumerate or he had just stolen the book from some nearby dealer and was trying to unload it fast before word got round. As soon as I began examining the book I realised, from the code pencilled in the back, that it had been taken from the Oxfam charity shop in Greene Street. I told the young man that it was a very interesting book, indeed, and that if he could leave it with me to examine further, I could almost certainly give him a good deal more than £12. He said okay, promised to return in an hour and headed out of the door. As soon as he'd disappeared I telephoned the Oxfam shop and said I'd just been offered one of their books, obviously stolen, at a very low price. "Impossible," said a rather snooty-sounding volunteer. "All of our best books are kept safely on a shelf behind the desk where I am presently . . ." She paused for no more than two seconds, then, "Oh, dear. May I send someone round to collect it, Mr. Bankes?"

I said she could, but that whomever she sent would have to show me proof of identity.

"There are a lot of thieves around these days, you see."

The scruff, of course, never returned to collect his book. And by the following morning, thanks to our book-thief grapevine, his description was being circulated throughout both booksellers' associations.

******

Book fairs, where local dealers come together periodically to display their wares publicly - (rather like artists exhibiting in a group show) - can be fertile territory for the recovery of stolen books. Most Bath bookdealers I've known, while browsing their colleagues' shelves at a fair, have suddenly spotted a book that was stolen from them - not by the colleague displaying it, but by the book thief that the colleague bought it from, (usually, in all innocence). Rightful ownership of the book can nearly always be established by a distinctive identification mark somewhere in its pages. (I, for example, always pencilled BB on page 51 of any book I offered at over £50.) And once that has been settled it is conventional practice for the purchaser of the stolen book to hand it back to its rightful owner in exchange for half the sum he paid the thief for it. What results is a kind of mutually shared misfortune, but at least neither dealer has lost everything, and after all, one can console oneself with the old shop keeper's adage, "Turn-over is turnover, however miserable."

But if the stolen book has not been purchased in all innocence, if the bookdealer knowingly pays £5 for a book worth £50 or £100, doesn't report the transaction, and then resells it at its real value, he is, in effect, complicit in the fencing of stolen goods and should be prosecuted. Or as Peter Goodden once put it to me: "Dealers who knowingly buy from pond life, should be thrown into the pond themselves!"

And so they should be. They not only corrupt the market and make all bookdealers look a bit suspicious, they actively encourage theft by making themselves known at pond level as a safe market for stolen books - and I say 'safe' because all the police can do is try to spot them on CCTV footage. (I've already described how effective that is.) And even if a corrupt dealer could be caught on tape doing business with a thief, there would then be the impossible task of proving he was knowingly complicit in handling stolen goods, when all he'd need do was throw up his hands and say, 'I made a mistake' or 'I was convinced the seller was the book's legitimate owner.' There is no way the police can disprove that. And as for failing to report an obviously dodgy transaction to the association grapevine - it isn't a crime.

******

The most troublesome, and indeed embarrassing, thieves in my experience, are those who hunt in pairs. Troublesome because they are professionals who can cost a bookseller a lot of money, embarrassing because they can make a bookseller look like an idiot. Thief A, usually well-dressed and well-spoken, will enter the shop, spend half an hour or more looking through books in, say, the Egyptology shelves, chat a bit, always charmingly, while opening and shutting books, then leave saying he is meeting a friend for lunch but will be back in an hour. Examination of the Egyptology section proves there are no books missing. Some time later Thief B enters, wearing a jacket, does a quick tour of the shelves vaguely in the area of the Egyptology section, then leaves again, saying something like, 'Sorry, couldn't find it.' It may then be an hour or more before I realise that the most expensive of all my Egyptology books has vanished. Picked off by Thief B, of course, who knew exactly where to find it because Thief A had told him.

******

Then there is the book plate thief - better described as the 'book plate swapper'. This nasty little con artist, again perfectly respectable-looking, will come innocently into the shop, buy a nicely illustrated, sometimes quite expensive book from me, then return a day or so later claiming that one of the plates is missing. Now I know perfectly well that when I collated and polished that book for display, all the plates were intact. So, do I risk unpleasantness by politely calling him a liar and asking him to leave? Or do I apologise and offer to buy the book back, at the price he paid for it? In effect, refund his money. To which he will say something like, "I'm sure it was a genuine mistake, Mr. Bankes, and I do like the book. Perhaps you could give me something back, say 50 per cent, then I will have bought a faulty book at a fair price, but one that I do like." At which point, knowing perfectly well what he's up to, my only choice is to say sweetly, that I don't sell books with missing plates, and must therefore insist on buying it back from him. Whatever he decides after that doesn't matter - I've lost a sale, and possibly, if he's already excised the plate for sale on its own, a perfect book. But the point is to keep him from ever coming back to the shop.

******

I mentioned earlier my decision to keep my most expensive books on two glass-fronted shelves behind my desk. The idea, obviously, to thwart light fingers. Anybody who wanted to look at those books would have to ask me to take them down from the shelf and then agree to look at them on my desk where there was no risk of them being damaged. Fool proof, or so I thought!

One morning, a well-dressed man in his late 40's approached my desk and asked if I could recommend a really nice present for his boss who was retiring from the firm, and had always been terribly kind to him. He thought a book up to say, £500, if the subject were appropriate, was roughly what he was after. "That, for example," he said, pointing at one of the books behind me, a beautifully bound folio volume entitled *Costumes of China*, which included, despite the title, some quite horrific illustrations of corporal punishments. I unlocked the glass doors, took it down for him and opened it on my desk. "Yes," he said, turning over a few pages, "this is the sort of thing. May I look at some of the others in those shelves?"

A pleasant 20 minutes went by while I took down more books from behind the desk, each of which he looked at with great interest before asking to see another. The pile of expensive books on my desk had grown to seven or eight, all of them under serious consideration, and I was just turning away to take down the next one he'd asked to see, when he looked at his watch and asked where he could get a good, quick lunch. I pointed in the direction of Mike Robinson's delicatessen, said the sandwiches were excellent, and he said these were exactly the sort of thing he was looking for, that he'd make up his mind over a bite to eat and be back within half-an-hour. When an hour had gone by, I began putting the pile of books back in their secure shelves. All except for one, that is - the deluxe edition, vellum-bound Arthur Rackham's *English Fairy Tales*, the most expensive of the lot - which was no longer there. I telephoned Mike at the Delicatessen: "Nope, no one like that has come in. Do you want me to ring if he turns up?"

I thanked him and said not to bother. By now, I calculated, he'd be on the 2:07 to Oxford (A lot of expensive books stolen in Bath end up in Oxford.) and chortling happily: *So grateful to that nice Mr. Bankes for not bothering to put back each book before getting down the next. And for so helpfully turning away from me when he did that.*

May he rot forever in a beautiful library full of vellum-bound Arthur Rackhams, where every time he touches a book a bell rings and Rottweilers bound out to gnaw his legs.

Unlike art theft or jewellery theft, where specific items of known value are targeted, and a buyer will have been lined up in advance (or indeed, may have 'commissioned' the theft himself), stealing books from a second hand book shop is in most cases an opportunistic, haphazard affair. The thief rarely has much idea of what he will find on the shelves when he walks in, or what its value may be, or where to offload later whatever he gets away with. Unlike art or jewellery thieves, his aim will rarely be to make a big killing, but merely to get away with enough to feed himself, or his habit for a day or two, or if he's lucky, for a week. The more expensive the titles he steals, the more he can expect (or hope) to get for them. But only up to a point. No experienced book thief would be dumb enough to steal a *Gutenberg Bible*, say, or a first Shakespeare folio and then expect not to be caught when he tried to sell it on. Unlike valuable art, you can't really hold a valuable book for ransom (who would pay it?), and unlike stolen jewellery, you can't re-cut or melt down a valuable rare book and resell it in unidentifiable new forms. And anyway, a really famous stolen book would be refused by any self-respecting fence as, 'Too hot to handle, mate'. If, by chance, such a treasure did come his way, he would almost certainly turn the thief in for a fat reward, and retire to the Bahamas under an assumed name.

Still, experienced book thieves will, within reason, always go for the priciest targets they believe they can safely sell on, and nothing aids them so much in that pursuit as the jolly bookdealer's habit of pricing each of his books in pencil on an early fly leaf. (An unavoidable habit, even a small shop like Bankes Books, will have something like 7,000 to 8,000 titles on its shelves at any one time, and the only way to keep track of the prices of all those books is to write them in pencil at the front.) What this leads to is thieves, pretending to be customers, being able to price a great number of books in a fairly short time, and then steal the most valuable. If I spot a 'customer' going through books this way - only checking fly leaves before going on to another book - I know I'm in the presence of a thief and can deal with the situation accordingly; usually a good natured, "Did you plan to pay for those books you've tucked under your coat?" (… in your rucksack? … down your trousers?) will do the trick. The books will be replaced on my desk, sometimes sheepishly, sometimes angrily, and the thief will not return. In most cases, that is. If, however, as I described earlier, the thief answers, "What books?" and brazens it out, there is very little a poor bookseller can do except watch his stolen goods go out of the door, contact the association grape vine, and hope his lost books find their way home again one day.

Alternatively, one could keep Rottweilers on the premises, I suppose.

******

And finally, the most outrageous example of bare-faced cheek I have ever met with at the hands of a book thief. Since my days in the IT business, I have had a particular interest in Sir William Petty, the man generally agreed to be the father of the art of statistical analysis. I was therefore pleased and perplexed in equal measure when a man I can best describe as a large, leering drunk walked into the shop, asked if I bought old books, and when I said yes, placed a good copy of Petty's *Observations Upon the Dublin-Bills of Mortality* on my desk. It was a book worth a great deal of money, and when I opened it to the second fly leaf I saw £6000 clearly pencilled on the top left corner. The writing was not mine, but the book had a familiar look to it, and I wondered if it was the same copy I'd sold a year or so ago at the London Book Fair to a fellow antiquarian whose writing, when I looked at it more closely, might well have been his. I recalled then that my copy had a handsome, rather unusual bookplate to the front pastedown page, but when I looked there, the page was blank, with no bookplate of any description. Obviously, it hadn't been my book. But then neither, just as obviously, did it belong to the man who was showing it to me now.

"This is very nice," I said to him. "Very nice, indeed. May I ask how you come to have it?"

He leant across my desk, stinking of cheap beer: "Gorrit from a fren, dint I?" he leered, and then actually winked at me.

"I see," I said, suddenly realising he thought I was one of those despicable dealers who was known to buy from thieves. Followed by - wondering why in the world he would think that, then finally, wondering if the old 'May-I-keep-this-for-an-hour-to-examine-it-more-closely' trick would work on him. As I started to close the book, a shaft of light from outside crossed the pastedown and I saw scratch marks just where the bookplate I remembered would have been. Clearly, an amateur (for which read 'the thief who'd stolen the Petty from my colleague') had removed the bookplate and then clumsily scratched off the gum used to stick it in place.

"And how did your friend come to have it?" I asked, lightly.

"Why do you want to know that?" he returned, beginning to sound a little belligerent.

"Because if we look on page 51," I said, "I think we may find that your friend and I have the same initials. Wouldn't that be a strange coincidence . . . ?" I leafed through the pages to 51, then turned the book to show him the BB I'd pencilled in the gutter after I'd acquired it at auction nearly three years before. But it was too late to discover if Mr. Leery found the coincidence as strange as I did - he was already out of the shop and running away towards Brock Street.

CHAPTER SIX: FAIRS & RINGS

"Kicking a bookseller in the ribs can lead to expulsion."

Book fairs provide a valuable opportunity for a shop owner or market trader to show his most enticing titles to a wider than usual audience in company (and in competition) with his peers. When held outside the area where he normally trades, fairs also provide a chance to meet new customers, new colleagues, new dealers and new contacts all in one place over two or three whirlwind days of selling, buying, bargaining, hustling, bragging, gossiping, socialising, along with a lot of other 'ings' - except (usually) sleeping.

The annual Bath book fair, held over a long week-end each September in one of the city's famous exhibition spaces - often the Assembly Rooms or the Guildhall - is considered to be the Jewel in the South West's Crown. I took a stall there the year we opened Bankes Books and continued to do so, without fail, for the next 22 years. I also showed occasionally at some of the lesser jewels - notably Bristol, Shepton Mallet and Wells book fairs - but not that often, and not with that much enthusiasm. Moving boxes of books in and out of the car, driving for miles, setting up the stall, then packing up at day's end and driving home again is frankly exhausting - doubly, so if it has proved to be a completely wasted day. Some dealers, though, put themselves through that struggle every Saturday hoping to sell even a few books at whatever fair they can get to. And there is always a fair being held somewhere within striking distance; sometimes even two or three. Choosing the right fair for selling well will depend largely on whether it is being run by a reputable organisation - the PBFA, for example - or a potentially dodgy independent group who may not be above allowing trading in books of questionable provenance.

Being known to have a stall at some book fair or other every week does seem to indicate a trader lodged permanently at the bottom of the pecking order. Sometimes it's true - but not always. Many of the larger, more successful dealers will take a stall at an established fair simply to look for bargains before the public arrives. Because fairs must open their doors an hour or so early to allow for setting up stalls, those who have set up quickly enough can sacrifice a mug of coffee and a chat with colleagues in order to walk around looking for bargains on their fellow-exhibitors' shelves; they will think themselves most unlucky if they don't find at least one very good book being offered at far too low a price, which they can take back to their shops and sell for a considerable profit - or indeed, sell for a profit right there. Beginner's ignorance - which you may remember I suffered from rather badly in my first Wednesday Market days - is the key element in bagging such bargains. My first time at Wells, for example, I sold a first edition of C.S. Lewis' *The Silver Chair* in a very good dust wrapper for £10 at the beginning of the day - and before closing time was mortified to see it displayed successively by three other dealers at £30, £60, and £100. This, of course, was before Lewis became hot property in the world of children's books. But those other dealers knew what I didn't – that a Lewis craze was coming, not thanks to clairvoyance, but because their customers had already begun asking for his works. (Peter Goodden once told me that customers provided one of our most accurate insights into future market trends and should therefore be cozened with great care. Actual love, however, was considered a bit excessive by serious bookdealers.)

Our third year at the Bath book fair turned out to be a modest triumph; I sold four, very rare, very expensive geography books to a London collector who was a world expert in that field, and later on picked up half-a-dozen first edition bargains to fill out my depleted Restoration Poetry and Drama shelves. Then one evening about a week after the fair closed, Maryanne and I were chatting over coffee about the possibility of doing Wells again next year, when each of us said simultaneously, "I wonder why there's never been a fair in Bradford-on-Avon?" and "Wouldn't it be convenient if there were a fair in Bradford-on-Avon?" To which the simultaneous answer was, "Good question." Followed by Maryanne's, "I'm going to bring it up at the PBFA bash next week."

Maryanne and I had been members of the PBFA for more than three years now, and had been wondering what she and I might contribute to the association in a constructive way, as other members did - something more concrete than helping to serve coffee and donuts when the Bath fair was on. We'd decided, after our Bradford-on-Avon chat, that our good deed should be helping to organise and run a book fair there in the autumn - if the PBFA approved, of course. In pursuit of which decision we drove over to Bradford the next day, ascertained that the public hall near the bridge in the town centre would be available the last weekend in October, found out its hiring price and insurance costs, plus availability of parking, plus health and safety requirements and went to the PBFA's South West Area meeting two days later armed with notes. When the chair called, "Any Other Business," Maryanne stood up and proposed that she and I set up and run a Bradford-on-Avon book fair at the end of October. After she'd read out the essential details we'd collected, there was some discussion about whether such a fair would take trade away from Bath book-dealers, and more particular concerns about train times, car parking, public toilets and baby changing facilities. One woman, a dealer in illustrated miniatures, wanted to know if we would allow dogs into the hall during the fair.

"At Shepton Mallet last year," she said, almost tearfully, "someone brought a toy poodle in and it peed on my decorated edges."

But response was largely positive, and in the end we were

given the go-ahead to organise the first ever officially sanctioned Brad-ford-on-Avon book fair. We asked for help and advice from everyone there, and were greatly encouraged by the enthusiastic response of our fellow association members - in no small part, Maryanne insisted, because they really were keen on the idea of a Bradford-on-Avon fair and not, as I kept suggesting, because they were terrified we'd disgrace the whole of the South West Area by creating a shambles.

At any book fair, large, small, new or long-standing, the criti-cal issue in determining shambles or success is iron-clad, pre-paid, stall-holder bookings. Once our fair had been approved, the PBFA added its name to the list of venues in the booking form it sends out each Spring to all of its members. The form includes the dates, loca-tions, average take from the previous year, and stall-holder fees for ev-ery fair scheduled for the upcoming year. The stall-holder fee, which must be paid in advance, will be used by the organisers to defray costs. We estimated we must have 19 firm bookings to cover our basic costs at Bradford, 25 to make a small profit (and make the hall look reasonably full), and 30 or more to create a successful fair. If we'd got it badly wrong in estimating the minimum number of exhibitors we'd need, then we would be very unpopular indeed with Head Office (though it was unlikely we should actually have our heads chopped off).

Even so, the Chandor family had a nervous summer waiting for bookings to come in. With two months to go only five had booked. With six weeks to go, only eleven. Should we have written a more enticing description of the venue? Would it have helped to point out that the Moulton bicycle was designed and manufactured in Brad-ford-on-Avon? Or that its citizens read constantly as they commuted to and from London? That the town, which boasted a tiny, beautifully restored Saxon church and a world-renowned medieval tithe barn had once been called 'The Book Capital of the West?' (Or so Mary-anne assured me.)

Then as October approached we were finally told that 28 brave souls had booked for the fair. Next came a fierce encounter with the council's Keeper of the Diary. No, we could not put up any posters until the day before the fair; no, we could not put up direction signs around the town until three days before the fair, no we most certainly could not string a banner across the main street advertising a book fair - this was Bradford-on-Avon, for heaven's sake - Medieval gem of West Wiltshire!

The direction signs essential to any enterprise like this were helpfully provided by PBFA Head Office; so a week before the fair was scheduled to open, armed with a bright orange highlighter and a large scale map of Bradford-on-Avon, we marked what we believed were the most useful places to put them up, and then carefully calculated the number which would need arrows pointing left, right and straight ahead. This was a lot more difficult than we expected; first, because we could never agree on which was left and which was right, and second, because we had no idea if there would be a convenient lamppost where we had selected our sign sites.

But we faced up bravely to these little difficulties, finished marking our map, and then prepared a press release to be sent to all the local newspapers, radio stations, and the nice people at Points West TV. Our press release included the gob-smacking news that one exhibitor would be showing a first edition of *Through the Looking-Glass* with the 'outgrave' misprint for 'outgrabe', and even more exciting, that Leo McKern (aka Rumpole of the Bailey, himself) had agreed to open the fair for us - a coup of coups that of course would bring thousands running. PBFA central office, meanwhile, had undertaken the printing of advertising leaflets which we planned to have urchins stick under the windscreen wipers of every parked car in town. Cars left all day in the car park probably belonged to commuters we reasoned, who might be pleased not only to have something different to do on an October Saturday, but who could simultaneously refresh their stock of reading material for the train ride into London the following Monday.

We feared it would rain, of course, and like picnickers all over the world, studied conflicting weather forecasts every hour on the day before the fair. Uncharacteristically, I sprang out of bed at six o'clock the next morning - and very nearly sprang back in again. It wasn't raining; in fact it was bright and sunny. A good fry-up prepared me for the day, however arduous it might prove to be, and I arrived at our venue just before eight o'clock, having followed our direction signs with perfect ease. The car park was almost empty when I drove in, and I parked near the gently sloping ramp leading into the hall. The hall manager, bless her lisle stockings, was there to let me in, and the first thing we did was make an urn of coffee in the little kitchen at the back of the room. I had forgotten to bring milk, but the thrice-blessed manager hadn't. "You'll find a whole-cow's worth in the fridge," she said sweetly, "and sugar on the kitchen counter beside the urn, with mugs and spoons."

I unloaded the car after my first delicious mug and was just finishing setting up our shelves near the exit, when I heard the comforting rumble of trolleys rolling up the ramp outside, heralding the arrival of our first stall-holders.

The early arrivals were terribly kind in helping me put right trivial mistakes I'd made in marking out the stall locations the night before, specifically not putting them in the best positions possible. There was no difficulty in correcting this; it simply meant picking up the label for Bloggs Books and substituting their own for it. If Bloggs wanted the best place, they reasoned, he should have come earlier.

Equipment required for a fair is similar to that needed for a weekly market: half-a-dozen folding shelves (the famous 'thumb-pinchers' which close flat and open to provide three shelves); a table, with a suitable cloth cover (used to display open books and to staunch the blood when a folding shelf turns nasty); wedges to keep the shelves stable on an uneven floor; two dozen plastic boxes, each of which should carry about twenty books; the books to fill the boxes, which should number about five hundred in total for a fair of this size; a trolley on which to wheel the laden boxes into the fair; lots of loose change in a cigar box or brightly coloured bowl; and a very strong back! (Indeed, Bookseller's Back is so common among stall-holders at fairs that customers frequently have to step over their supine bodies to get to the books they want. Customer protocol requires that stepping over a bookseller who is resting his back this way while simultaneously guarding his books, must be done with great care - kicking a bookseller in the ribs can lead to expulsion - and should, ideally, be accompanied by a word or two of genuinely-felt sympathy; "Get up, for goodness' sake, you lazy slob!" is not acceptable and may also lead to expulsion.)

Finally, a stall-holder must possess enough faith and grit to sustain him through six or seven hours of watching his books being pawed over by grubby fingers, reviled by ignoramuses, and then rudely shoved back onto their shelves un-purchased. Worse still, the stall-holder offering books that nobody even wants to look at, must be prepared to stand lonely as a cloud for hour after hour, wearing a cheerful expression, never being offered a kindly word - or even a rude one - until sometime late in the afternoon, as packing up is about to begin, that little woman in plimsolls and a straw hat who appears at every provincial book fair in Christendom, rushes up to ask if he has Volume 4 of the *Rainbow Annual*. Which of course he doesn't.

******

By nine o'clock there was a steady rumble of trolleys bringing in books. Shelves started going up quickly, and the coffee was going down well - especially for those who had come from distant parts. We'd arranged for some students from Bath University to act as porters for older exhibitors who needed help moving boxes, and by nine-thirty a hall that had been empty an hour earlier had been miraculously transformed into a lively, colourful book fair.

At quarter to ten I was able to announce to our exhibitors that a very promising queue was forming outside the main entrance, and that Mr. McKern was standing just outside the side entrance rehearsing his speech with Mrs. McKern. Five minutes later Maryanne ushered them into the hall and gave them coffee and doughnuts while I went across to the main doors and pushed them open. The crowd that entered appeared to number a hundred or so already, and because the weather was good and everyone was dressed in Indian Summery clothes, the sense of festivity created was quite wonderful - and certainly gratifying. At ten o'clock, the magic manager handed me a big, silver, hand-bell of the 'oyez, oyez, all rise' sort, which I rang ostentatiously to much applause, and then invited Mr. McKern to step forward and do the honours. He welcomed everyone with great solemnity, made a small joke about the stocks that had been set up outside next to the mediaeval prison on the bridge to accommodate those who failed to buy books, and declared the inaugural Bradford-on-Avon book fair open.

"So far so good," I said to Maryanne, when the McKerns had taken their leave.

"At least it's happening," she replied.

"You didn't think it would?"

"I did," she laughed. "You're the one who didn't."

The crowd kept growing. They all seemed to be having a good time. All the stall-holders seemed to be selling - Bankes Books, included. By noon, as far as we could tell, there had not been a single disaster - not even a spilled coffee. By 5 p.m., the only downbeat moment in the whole day came when I had to announce that England were doing appallingly against Australia in the Test match. Half an hour before closing time Sarah went around handing out little slips of paper on which exhibitors were asked to write down the total of their takings so we could estimate how well we'd actually done, and then pass the news on to PBFA Head Office. She collected these just before the doors closed at six, and a moment later the wind-down noises of trolleys coming back in, unsold books being re-loaded into boxes, and what sounded to Maryanne and me to be a lot of cheerful stall-holder voices exchanging anecdotes about their successes. I was touched by the number of exhibitors who delayed their departures long enough to come across to Maryanne and thank us for arranging such an excellent fair. But as I've been trying to make clear all along, booksellers are a thoroughly pleasant lot. Despite what people say.

******

On the other hand, they are not always as thoroughly observant as they might be. For example: one hot afternoon at a busy book fair in Brighton, I had walked away from my stand to chat to another bookseller at his stall not far away. I kept a good watch on my stall and was outraged to see a short man in a mackintosh open his briefcase and drop in a book. Oh, Lord. What was I to do now? Should I just let him get away with it? He wasn't a big man, but was I hero enough to chase him and bring him to the ground in a glorious rugger tackle? Supposing the chase brought the surrounding stalls crashing to the ground, books all over the place, change sent flying, angry booksellers growling, "Who's going to pay for this?" No heroics, then. Time instead for sweet reason backed by the moral strength of keen observation. I walked over to the mackintosh-clad man and said:

"Excuse me, sir but would you like to buy that book?"

"What book would that be?" he said.

"The book you just put in your briefcase."

"No," he said, scowling now, "I would not like to buy that book."

"I think you'd better give it to me in that case," I said.

"Now why would I want to do that?" he said

"If you'll open your briefcase, I'll show you why."

He did, and produced the very book I'd seen him put there not a minute before - which somehow had transformed itself into a worn, black leather notebook bound with a red rubber band.

"Oh," I said.

"Oh, indeed," he said.

"And now," I said, "I suppose you're going to tell me you were making note of books of mine that interested you."

"I was, as a matter of fact," he said. "Not so sure now though, Mr. Bankes"

"Actually," I said, "it's Fawlty . . . "

******

Every year, Maryanne and I took a stall at one or other of the several big London book fairs that were held each June. For many of those years we made a special point of showing at the Café Royal organised by our old friend Gerry Mosdell. Later we would stay with him when he began holding his two-day fairs at the Eden Hotel in South Kensington. Choosing that venue was typically clever of Gerry, who realised that as the hotel was quite near the Kensington Olympia (London's largest exhibition venue at that time) it was likely that exhibitors at the ABA's flagship fair there would look in at Gerry's fair in the hope of finding a bargain or two which could then be translated to their stands at Olympia.

The London June fairs in the 1990's were happy occasions for buyers and sellers alike, with wads of notes changing hands all round the exhibition rooms, and, although it was expensive for those who had to stay overnight in London, I never heard anyone express a louder complaint than the occasional "not as good as last year".

All fairs can have slow moments, just as all fairs can have frenetic ones. During a quiet moment at the Café Royal, Maryanne suggested I should offer some of the exhibitors our early seventeenth-century copy of the works of Julius Caesar. The book had been through the wars a bit, as the Americans say, and was very nearly in three parts itself, but we still felt it deserved to find its way into the hands of one of the antiquarians showing here - if for no other reason than that we wanted to get rid of it. Always up for a challenge, I thought about strategy briefly, then delivered the famous line that ever delights the heart of any bookseller's partner: "I have a cunning plan." Which simply involved disguising myself as a punter by going to one of the stands furthest from ours (where I was sure I wouldn't be recognised as a dealer), and asking the stall-holder that classically idiotic question: "Excuse me, but do you buy books?" To which the dealer is always gagging to say, "No, stupid, I steal them!", but of course has to respond with some fawning bit of drivel like, "Yes, can I help you, sir?"

Now I have often noticed that when an ordinary punter is seen offering a book to a dealer at a fair, a smouldering jealousy breaks out among the other dealers nearby, and a look of cherubic smugness suffuses the face of the chosen one. And so it was this time. I was offered a price for the Julius Caesar. I said, "Oh, is that enough?" and then, "Perhaps that man next to you could offer me a bit more . . ." And within minutes, while the would-be assassins ground their teeth in fury, I'd been offered a price I knew was reasonable for us and the Julius Caesar had found its new home.

******

On a house call once, I bought an entire small library that

included a number of books in Hebrew. I'd no idea what they were about, and hadn't found means of discovering if they were worth anything, so they sat in a corner of our basement at home, unpriced, but regularly dusted. During packing up for a London fair one June, I found we were short of books by 20 or so, so I snatched up the Hebraic group and added them to the boxes. Arrived at the Cafe Royal, we found a good stall near the entrance, and decided to ask a fellow exhibitor, who often showed books in Hebrew, whether he thought my little group was worth anything. Books on shelves, and with Maryanne in charge, I went off to park the car. I came back half-an-hour later to find Maryanne deep in discussion with a man in a black Homburg and Orthodox Jewish side-curls. As I approached our stall, Maryanne gave me a 'not just now' look and continued talking earnestly to the Jewish gentleman. While I watched from a distance, the man finally shrugged, produced a cheque-book, wrote with great care and then exchanged his cheque for all my Hebrew books which he carried away in a plastic bag.

I re-joined Maryanne who immediately rebuked, "What on earth do you mean, leaving me with a pile of unpriced illegible books? I had no idea what to do when he asked how much for the lot."

"Well, you seemed to have got on all right. What did you ask for it?"

"I didn't know what to ask, so I said £1000."

Good Lord, I thought. "Did he say yes?"

"He offered £200," Maryanne said, "and eventually we agreed on £500."

I was staggered. "I'd hoped for £10," I smiled, "but £500 will do."

I'm not quite sure what lesson I learned from this. Always price books immediately, however troublesome, is the right answer, I suppose. On the other hand, if I don't price the books, and Maryanne does the deal, look how much more we make!

******

A very close friend of ours, whom I'll call Jack Woodley, was an exhibitor at the Bradford-on-Avon fair, and in a quietish moment before the fair ended, he beckoned me over to his stall in a strangely sinister way.

"Look," he said, "You know James Wilson couldn't make it to the fair because he's in hospital. Nothing serious, but he won't be out until tomorrow and I can't very well ring him up if he's groaning on a bed in pain. I did speak to him yesterday, though, and he told me he particularly wanted to look at some crumbling Latin book Mary Williamson has found. She's on stall 34. Her price is £400, which is a bit steep for me. Would you be willing to take a look and go halves if you're interested? Jim says it's not listed in BAR or anywhere else he's looked it up, so I hope your Latin's as good as you've always pretended it is."

My Latin isn't all that good, but this book sounded intriguing, and especially so if Jack and James Wilson were both interested in it, since both were highly respected dealers and had a deserved reputation for knowing their stuff. I wandered across to Mary Williamson's stand and immediately spotted the big folio book lying on a table to one side. My Latin may be rubbish but I knew enough to identify it at once as a Polychronicon (a collection of all known things). It included a pretty basic map of the world with no North or South America shown, and was dated 1478 on the title page. What I was looking at, if it was legitimate, was an incunabulum; a so-called "cradle book" produced from hand-set wooden type before 1501, at the very birth of printing. Mary told me she'd bought it from a Vicar who knew no more about it than that it was old and in Latin. She also said she hadn't tried to collate it because frankly, she'd no idea how to begin; the book didn't appear in any reference she knew of. And, indeed, I'd never run across it in any reference I'd ever consulted. It was in decent condition, though, despite rather scruffy boards, and I thought, *go for it Chandor*, took out my cheque book and asked what her best price was.

"I'm sorry, Anthony, this one has to be £400." *Absolutely right, too*, I thought, wrote out the cheque and carried what might well prove to be a great find, a sleeper sleeping sounder than Rip van Winkle himself, gingerly back to Jack's stand. He seemed a bit disappointed that I'd paid full price, but said that after we'd cleared up when the fair was over - the 'we' included him of course - could Maryanne and I go with him to the Eight Bells round the corner to meet a few people and talk about the Poly-wossitsname we'd just bought?

I returned with the Polychronicon to our stand and showed it to Maryanne. One rarely sees Maryanne's eyes light up over anything other than a very good tennis stroke or a chocolate éclair from Fortnum's - but they lit up now. She looked carefully through the book page by page while I held my breath, then spent several minutes examining the map with a magnifying loop. I finally had to let my breath out and take another. Then another. And then: "I think it's all right," she said finally, and I breathed freely again.

"I assume Jack will want to put it into the Ring now," she said. "He owes us £200, and he'll be hoping to recover most of that from the divvy. We'll both go, and I'll bid up to, what do you think? Say £1000?"

"Do you think there will be that much competition for it?" I asked her uneasily.

"I don't think there'll be any," she said, "but why take a chance?"

There were seven other dealers in the Eight Bells, crouching round a big glass-topped table piled with books. Rory Smethwick took the role of auctioneer. In all, nine books had been entered for bidding; the Polychronicon was to be the last. The first eight raised a disappointing £170 among them. And when Rory called out "ancient ... incunabulum", no one showed any interest at all. Mainly because no one knew what it was. We waited. And waited. "Any bids at all?" Rory asked, finally. At which point Maryanne took a big breath and with no preliminaries said, "£800."

Instant smiles all round; the divvy would be worth something after all! Good old Maryanne, they all thought. And as no one made a counter-bid - why should they, still having no idea what the thing was worth? - the book was ours at what proved to be a very, very modest price. Why? Because two months later Maryanne took our Polychronicon to Christie's and sold it for £24,000.

Awake, van Winkle!

But I must digress to explain what actually happened when we went round the corner to the Eight Bells to put our

Poly-Whatsitsname into "The Ring". And I can do that most simply
with the following story: At one of the first auctions I attended, (when
I was still, admittedly, a babe in the woods), I was surprised to see a
number of fine, illustrated children's books go to extremely low bids.
The estimates in the auctioneer's catalogue were up to scratch, and
there was no lack of dealers in such books on hand. But all of the
lots went to only one of those dealers, and at prices that were clearly
much lower than seemed to me logical. I was then even more surprised - baffled, actually - when, at the end of the auction, someone I
regarded as a leading bookseller came up to me, thanked me for my
tact, and suggested I join 'the rest of us' in the car park. Thanked me
for what tact? I couldn't imagine. So, as I had not bought anything
that day, or even made a bid, and the offer of a get-together in a
parking lot didn't appeal greatly, I thanked him, got in my car and
left. I learned later that by not bidding for anything that day I had
unwittingly earned myself the right to a so-called 'divvy', and that by
declining to join 'the rest of us in the car park' I had narrowly avoided taking part in an illegal, but widely-practised price-fixing strategy
called 'the Ring'.

   The Ring, in simplest terms, comprises a group of dealers at an
auction (or occasionally a fair) who have agreed among themselves to
keep down the sale price of books they all want by not bidding against
one another. Once the books have been acquired by the designated
'winner', the members of the Ring meet and hold a second auction
conducted by the senior among them called The Ringmaster. This
time, of course, the books reach fair prices in competitive bidding.
Once they've all been sold, the sale money is put into a pool by the
Ringmaster, who first repays the 'winner' for his costs at the original
auction, and then divides whatever is remaining, called "the divvy",
equally among all of the Ring members. In this way, everyone gets
the book(s) he wants at a reasonable price, and with them a cash bonus which can sometimes amount to a considerable sum. (It certainly
did that evening at the Eight Bells thanks to Maryanne's £800 bid.)
The auctioneer, of course, loses some commission in this business.
But the real loser is the sweet little old lady with the shrinking pension
who put her beloved baby books into auction in hopes of making

enough to pay her winter heating bill and maybe have enough left
over to give her fluffy cat, Tiggles, a fresh sardine for his supper - because, 'Oh dear, Tiggles does so love a sardine.'

And it is because of that little old lady and people like her, that
The Ring has been illegal for more than fifty years, and why Ring
members no longer meet in car parks but repair instead, to some
discreet pub near the auction house to hold their second auctions.

******

As you can imagine, one does not make oneself popular at auctions by bidding knowingly against a Ring. My first encounter of this
kind happened at a local auction about a year after I'd declined that
invitation to the car park. At the viewing, I'd noticed two large, heavy
books posed together on a table that were being offered as a lot. One
was a Bible, scuffed and not worth more than £10. The other was a
Barclay's Dictionary, full of good eighteenth century plates and beloved of breakers (people who buy books in order to break the spines
to ease the removal of plates, which can then be sold individually, in
the case of Barclay's, for a total of £300 or more). The estimate for
the lot was a suspiciously low £30 – £50. I decided I could go to £150
tops and still come out ahead. Bidding opened at £20 and seemed to
be hesitating at £50. I bid £55 and was a little disappointed when
the auctioneer took a bid of £60 from someone directly behind me.
We bid against each other to £130 when a whisper behind me said,
"Ok, I'll see you afterwards." I turned round and recognised David
Latimer, a well-respected bookseller locally.

I settled my debt, moved to the collection point, and presented
my receipted account. My books were handed to me and I headed for
the exit. Suddenly, at my elbow, David Latimer muttered, "You owe
me £130."

I couldn't think how he had worked this out but replied firmly,
indeed very firmly, "I owe you nothing. We had no agreement before
the sale and if you wanted the Barclay you should have bid more for
it."

David, spitting with rage by then, growled, "We'll see about that," and stomped off to his own car. I left for mine and for a long time wondered what exactly it was we were going to see.

Nothing, as it turned out. Except I did notice, as the auctions went by month after month, that even when I didn't bid for anything, I was never again thanked for my tact by a well-known dealer. Or invited to join any groups anywhere.

******

Then one day we went to a small country auction in Cornwall – view in the morning from 10 o'clock with the sale at half-past two. We were still viewing at 2 o'clock, having taken rather longer to get there than we had expected. Oh, all right, then - I was a bit late getting up. Of interest to us were a number of miniature books in a single lot, an attractive set of Shakespeare in another lot, and then, in several lots, some good, eighteenth century flower books with hand-coloured plates. Looking at the plates, I remembered reading that the hand colouring in books of this vintage was often done by families, with Ma and Pa producing the larger areas of multiple colour, and the children each specialising in one particular colour or picture element (leaves for little Mabel, say, and twigs or grassy background for young Tommy). When the colouring-in was complete each copy would be carefully examined for accuracy of hue and consistency of tone. Once approved, the plates would then be collected at a specified time by a representative of the publisher, or 'stationer' as he was called in the eighteenth century, and the family would be paid its fee.

While we were examining these books, a man with a ginger moustache and a green hat came and stood beside me. I was just checking the condition of the pages in the last flower book when Ginger said, conspiratorially, "I shouldn't go for those."

"Why not?"

"Well, Mr. G likes those, you know."

I'd no idea who Mr. G was, but I was on foreign soil here, so all I said was "Thank you for telling me," and retreated with Maryanne to the safety of the tea tent.

"Do you think the G stands for Godfather?" I asked her in a

whisper.

"I'm sure of it," she whispered back.

"But I like those books," I said. "All of them."

"So do I."

When the sale started we immediately identified the terrible Mr. G. He was very tall and was wearing a white mackintosh, probably bought in America, with the collar turned up like Humphrey Bogart. He sat in the middle of the front row and when the miniature books were called, he was straight in, holding his catalogue high in the air so that everyone could see who was bidding. As the competition started to peter out, Maryanne and I stepped in, big city style, and soon it was us against him. Once he turned round and treated us to a quick scowl, but we went on to our maximum and got the miniatures. Next came the Shakespeare set, which we picked up quite cheaply (six volumes bound in dark green full calf, nothing special, but just right for the shop). Then the flower books were called and the trouble began. Mr. G outbid us for the first three lots when we reached our maximum and stopped. We went £20 above our maximum on the next lot at which point he abruptly stopped bidding – it was as if he knew exactly what we had decided to bid and ushered us up to it before stopping, himself. Then, to our surprise, we got the next two lots at well below our maximum. And the sale was over.

Ten minutes later, as we stood in the queue to pay our account, he approached us, looking huge in his American trench coat, and said, "Those flower books you got. There's just one I want. The first volume of the *Maund*. What will you take for it?"

He seemed pleasant enough, and I replied politely that we had bought the flower books for someone else. He sniggered, less politely, at this palpable evasion and asked if we had recently moved to Cornwall? No, I said, we're from Somerset. To which he jokingly replied that he hoped we weren't meaning to come often to Cornwall as he rather regarded the county as his territory. We smiled, got in the car and drove back to our B&B. It was explained to us later that evening by a couple who had also been at the auction that if Mr. G thought we were going to be serious competition at future auctions here, he would take steps to out-resource us at every lot we went for, bidding against us until he had pushed us past a reasonable price, even if the lot in question held no interest for him. He was, they said, the auction King in these parts, and he intended to retain his title - whatever it might cost him to drive people like us from his realm.

******

Bidding on the internet has to some extent diluted the power to bully, that petty provincial tyrants like this man can exercise. Nevertheless, the auction rooms can still assume the gritty menace of the bear-baiting arena at times. And for dealers of a gentler disposition seeking to stock their shops or market stalls, there is a gentler way.

CHAPTER SEVEN: HOUSE CALLS

"I have to thank the trolls."

Of a bookseller's four main sources of stock – fairs, auctions, runners and house calls - fairs are usually the least likely to produce an undiscovered treasure like our Polychronicon, but are good at turning up titles one might never see under other circumstances. Auctions usually include the greatest variety of titles and prices - and now that auctioneers sell to a much wider audience thanks to the Internet, most lots will go for fair prices despite the machinations of Rings and bullies. Runners, while almost never producing a treasure (unless come by questionably) are a ready source of popular bargains in the £1-to-£10 price range. But among the four, house calls are by far the most unpredictable - and hence the most exciting - where the dealer may cross the threshold to find the best offerings he has ever seen in his life, or just as frequently, the worst. Either way, though, house calls are always an adventure.

I made my first ever house call when Bankes Books had been open less than a week. It came in response to a request from one of my very occasional customers at the Wednesday Market who visited the shop one day to ask if I could be bothered looking at

'Grandfather's books'. I learned from experience fairly quickly, that house calls thus described usually meant either a large collection of barely saleable, bargain basement titles typified by the likes of the twenty-third paperback edition of *The Scarlet Pimpernel*; or, at the shelf's equally dreary other end, a highly specialised collection of junior chemistry magazines which might indeed be saleable to a few old anoraks but to no one else.

On this, my inaugural house call, however, I had no idea what I might encounter, or how properly to respond if everything I were shown was rubbish. The house, a late Queen Anne country manor, was located in the Wiltshire village of West Kington, and I was welcomed at the front door by a delightful family who offered me whisky or tea, both of which I declined, and who then led me to two piles of large, important-looking leather-bound volumes stacked with care on a handsome Georgian dining table. As I approached this table, jotting pad in hand, I noticed with some alarm that of the seven family members gathered around me, five were under fifteen - grandchildren or nephews, I presumed - and all pretty obviously hoping for a good share of the proceeds of Grandpa's valuable treasures . . .

. . . every one of which turned out to be either by or about the Victorian explorer Richard Burton. All were beautifully bound and all were in good condition. As I began going through the first of them, the father of the family asked if I'd mind naming a price for each rather than offering a portmanteau figure for them all. What I should have replied immediately was that in order to do that fairly, I would first have to research what each book had last made at auction. But as I was a complete beginner, and unwilling to expose myself to what I assumed would be taken for ignorance so early in a probably distinguished career as a bookseller, I said of course I would do that, then merely checked which books were first editions, which of them Burton had signed, which bore personal inscriptions, and then offered roughly half of what I felt each one would sell for. Faces steadily fell as I proceeded from one book to the next. And when I'd finished, the grandchildren and their parents thanked me for my time, but said regretfully that Grandfather probably would have wanted a bit more than I'd offered for most of the volumes. Out of kindness, however, (one couldn't mistake it) they did accept my offer of £200 for a very attractive twelve volume set of *One Thousand and One Nights* that Burton had translated, and with their jolly farewells trailing me from the front steps, I trudged out to my old Volvo with my books in a borrowed cardboard box thinking that this book business I'd gone into might be rather more complicated than I'd anticipated.

That night, without consulting the auction records, I collated the 12 books and priced them at twice what I had paid. The next morning I put them on display on the table beside my desk. Almost at once they were spotted by a Dutch dealer, whose eyes immediately sparkled, and I decided that the evening before had not been a complete waste after all - especially when he paid full price for the set without even asking if that were the best I could do. I can't recall how exactly I discovered what I should have been asking for Burton's translation, (it's called selective, ego-salving amnesia), but the Dutchman did keep coming back every six months or so, invariably asking if I had any more of those Burtons to sell. He usually bought other books on each visit, so I decided to regard the set as a loss leader - like a case of cheap lager in a supermarket. Cunning psychology.

******

In fact it's easy to make fearful blunders on house calls; mainly because one can't research in advance the approximate value of the books one will be shown. (Taking a tablet such as an iPad® helps with this, but there is the new danger that the seller will ask you to look up every book he has, and will expect you to pay the full price of the most expensive copy quoted.) On the other hand, splendid coups can also be made in all innocence if the seller is equally ignorant of his books' values. The truth is, some of my best ever buys were made at house calls simply because the seller had accepted far too little for something I didn't realise was very much better than I'd initially thought. But as often as that happened, the opposite also happened; my ignorance of a book's true value, allied to the fear of overpaying for something I wasn't sure about, resulted occasionally in my missing a great bargain - as in the case of a certain Mr. Lawson.

About a year after I opened the shop, a man calling himself Lawson came in and, after looking around for ten minutes or so, asked if
I could come to his home that evening to look at some books. The
house was out past Weston; hidden, as they always seem to be, behind
the proverbial 'hedge that ends just before the Slow sign that might
be concealed by shrubbery this time of year - you can't miss it'. After
three tries, the house one couldn't miss eventually revealed itself, and
Mr. Lawson, seeming oddly uneasy, led me to an unheated, rather
shabbily furnished sitting-room where I saw a lot of hard back books
piled on a large round table. I reckoned there were about seventy in
all, all of them modern, most of them missing their dust wrappers.
I started going through them and soon realised to my surprise that
nearly all were first editions and that most had been signed by their
authors on the title page: James Joyce was there, D. H. Lawrence,
T. E. Lawrence, A. A. Milne, Rudyard Kipling, Hemingway, Scott
Fitzgerald, Katherine Ann Porter, Jennifer Johnston, Ford Maddox
Ford, Ezra Pound - indeed, almost any author you could name who
had written an important book since the beginning of the twentieth
century. If Maryanne had been with me I'd have had no trouble assigning value to the entire collection - modern firsts being one of her
fields of expertise. But it wasn't mine - and the dreariness of the room
coupled with Mr. Lawson's evident nervousness made me wonder
suddenly if the signatures of all those famous men and women might
not be forgeries. Suppose Mr. Lawson spent his days tracking down
first editions of famous modern books and his evenings carefully forg-
ing the signatures of their authors? And didn't I seem to remember
that James Joyce signed his books on the last page? And Kipling on
the first fly leaf, not the title page? And Hemingway not at all? Had I,
the newest bookseller on the block, been targeted by a dastardly forg-
er as the easiest mark in Bath? Would word go round the bookshops
and market stalls tomorrow that the notorious Mr. Lawson had made
yet another killing - and guess who the pigeon was this time!

So I worked out the value of the books as first editions only - not
embellished with those famous signatures - and firmly made my offer,
asking whether he wanted cash or a cheque?

"Just a minute," he squeaked. "That's not nearly enough money. I'm disappointed, Mr. Bankes. I'm outraged, in fact. Perhaps you ought to leave now before I lose my temper!"

What would you have done? Say you hadn't noticed the signatures? Claim the absence of dust wrappers always affected value adversely? Admit you had doubts about the seller's probity? Call the police? What I did, in fact, was head for the door expressing the obviously insincere hope that he would do better elsewhere, and drove home feeling rather grubby.

I never did discover if those signatures were legitimate. And I never ran across any of those books in auction or on the shelves of a fellow Bath bookdealer. Modern firsts signed by their authors, unless accompanied by an inscription - "Good stuff, Ezra, keep it up!" signed "Tom" for example - aren't, generally speaking, worth that much more than unsigned modern firsts. But seventy together, if the signatures were legitimate, would certainly have added up to a pretty good bargain. So I'm just as happy not to have discovered how smart or foolish I was on that house call. Or so I prefer to tell myself.

******

Sometimes people who have asked you to come to their house to buy their books don't really want to sell. I was once welcomed by an old woman, Mrs. Delmer, with a strong 'no nonsense' English face who sat me down on a leather armchair and said:

"Look, I have two grandsons and apart from a very little money, all I've got left to leave to them are my books and the chairs you and I are sitting on. But to avoid a fight after my death, I'd like to leave two bookshelves full of books, one for Andrew and one for Siegfried. Could you sort these out so that the contents are more or less equal in value?"

I thought of explaining that my association insisted I charge for valuations, but before doing that I looked at the books on the four shelves. This immediately presented another problem: there were a dozen really good books about Bath. As a collection, they were worth more than all the others put together. I explained this to Mrs. Delmer.

Rather surprisingly, she beamed at me.

"Promise not to tell, but Andrew is the only one who's shown any interest in my Bath books. And I agree with you that it would be a shame to break up the collection. The fact is, I rather favour Andrew. So he gets the Bath books and Siegfried can do what he likes with the others. Now, Mr. Bankes, you haven't exactly valued the books, but I owe you for your time. How much?"

I couldn't very well ask for one of the Bath books, so we agreed that the cup of tea was good payment for all the strenuous work I'd done - and I left having enjoyed the visit hugely and the outcome no less.

******

If I were asked to advise someone on how to make a house call, I suppose that, along with a thousand other facetious booksellers, I would say, "Ring the doorbell, and wait." (We booksellers, as you can see from the above, and earlier examples of our repartee, do enjoy a most exquisitely refined sense of ironic humour; pity no one outside the circle seems to share it.) Joking aside, if I am asked how to make a successful house call, the first rule is to understand that you cannot predict what you will be shown or how your host will respond to any offers you make, so prepare yourself to be mentally flexible, unwaveringly patient, and ready to offer whatever help you may perceive to be necessary. For many people inviting you to assess and perhaps buy their books (for reasons that are frequently less than happy ones), those books may be like surrogate children to them. For others, reaction to your presence in their houses, even though they invited you, may equate to a guard dog's feeling about the postman at the front door. It is a sound first step to be ready to *like* what you are shown. And even if you don't like it, never say so. If you can't fake sincerity, then perhaps you'd be better suited to a career where sincerity is actually frowned upon - banking, for example.

Talking down, or otherwise denigrating a book to justify a low offer, is always to be avoided. (If you meet someone new, by analogy, you do not tell him his suit fits badly and he has unpleasant breath as a means of avoiding inviting him to tea.) Common politeness insists that we leave such comments unspoken, even though we long to make them, and in the same way we booksellers must hold back similar comments about someone's books. If you notice, in flicking the pages, an ugly ink mark, hold the book open at that page for a few seconds so that it is obvious you have seen it, but do not say anything. And if there is an ugly tear to the dust wrapper, say, "Of course, these are often a bit scruffy. But better the wrapper than the book, is our motto."

It may be that these points will have to be returned to later if, for example, the seller says, "But in Fotheringham's catalogue the very same book as mine is offered at very nearly three times what you are offering."

To which a suitably polite reply might be, "I expect that would have been for a fine copy, with a fine wrapper, no ink stains and a good appearance. And I believe I did say at the outset that I pay only half what I am going to sell a book for. Fotheringham, I happen to know, still has his copy so he won't want another, but if you did offer yours to him I expect he'd make a lower offer than mine."

If this fractious client counters with, "I think I'll just find out about that, myself!" simply bow politely and make for the door. There are a lot more books out there in the big wide world, and you will surely be offered a better copy than his sooner or later.

******

As time went by, my reputation as 'the man to ask round to look at one's books' steadily grew until I found I was frequently being asked to make two or three house calls a week. In part, I suppose, this was because people felt they could trust a bald man of a pleasing roundness. But perhaps more to the point, because I seemed to have earned something of a reputation for over-paying. By 'seemed', however, I don't mean I was being naive in my pricing. My over-paying was not, in fact, excessive, nor was it accidental. By becoming known as 'that jolly chap who always offered a bit more for Grandfather's books than the other chaps', I had become, in effect, the default dealer people automatically contacted when they needed to sell up unwanted books and even whole libraries. Which meant first chance to buy some wonderful books that those other chaps would have given eye teeth for, and which also repaid my 'naive' generosity many times over.

But, of course, no privilege comes without a price. Quite often, I would be invited to houses described as being 'just a mile or two outside Bath.' It was reaching these houses, always at night, that taught me the true meaning of the term, 'a country mile'. The mile or two promised would invariably mean five or six driven in pitch darkness along narrow, closely hedged-in lanes - with pot holes, naturally - trying to spot the white gate, one couldn't miss - but just as with Mr. Lawson, always did the first time. Still, none of this mattered if there were good books to be acquired and I could come away with a lighter pocket but a fuller car.

There were, however, several kinds of visits to be avoided, if avoidance could be managed without giving offence. One of these is the retired school teacher who has marvellous books that he truly loves, but admits, *after* you've arrived at his digs out past the cemetery that he's never been able to afford decent copies. Another is the sweet old lady who has several hundred copies of *Woman's Own* and *Woman's Weekly* as well as a pristine copy of the *Daily Mail Souvenir* edition of the Royal Wedding lovingly preserved in cling wrap.

Generally speaking, people who asked me to make a house call would innocently reveal with their first few words whether what they had to offer would be of interest to Bankes Books. I could then make a polite excuse if they weren't, and that would be that. But I did once almost make a very costly mistake following that strategy.

A white-haired, very vigorous woman in her late 60's named Madison, marched into the shop shortly before closing time one afternoon saying, "Can you come straight away please? My husband has died recently, his books are very valuable, and I need some money rather quickly. Can you come now? It's only just round the corner."

Accurately predicting that her 'just around the corner' meant at least half a mile away, but attracted by the 'very valuable' part, I said I would be at her door in an hour's time, closed the shop at five, and walked up through St. James's Square to her house in one of Bath's finest Georgian terraces, Cavendish Crescent. The sitting-room she led me into was lined with books, floor to ceiling, but my spirits sank when I began to examine them and realised they were all inexpensive editions of popular – hence widely available – nineteenth and twentieth-century novels; the sort of books one might pick up for a pound at a charity shop or a village fête. I spent nearly two hours looking at every book on the shelves, and eventually, as I reached the last, had to say, "I'm so sorry, I'm afraid I can't buy anything I've seen here."

Her eager, hopeful face crumpled pathetically, and I felt awful.

"But Mr. Madison promised me they were valuable."

"I wish I could say that were true," I said, feeling genuinely sorry, "but I can't."

I was just heading for the front hall, when she said, "Wait, please . . ." leant over the back of a sofa and hauled up a Tesco's bag with eight or nine more books in it. "At least take these with you to pay for your time, Mr. Bankes. I don't want them in the house."

I took the bag from her, lifted out the first book, and found myself holding a copiously illustrated copy in French of *Le Phallus*. The next book was one of the earliest treatises on statistics published in English. I went through the rest, one by one, all but salivating over the bookseller's equivalent of having unearthed the Holy Grail. A quarter of an hour later, having accepted the cup of tea I'd declined earlier, I sat back on the sofa, totted up the figures I'd scribbled on the back of an envelope, and said, "I can offer you £3650 for these."

"Oh, I'm so glad," she said. "I'd have showed you them earlier, but I didn't realise you sold dirty books in your shop."

"I don't," I assured her. "These aren't dirty books, Mrs. Madison; quite the opposite, in fact."

"Oh," she said, "then I suppose *they* must be the ones he meant were valuable. Not those others," and she waved a hand around at the shelves and laughed. "I am a ninny, aren't I?"

Her pleasure was charming; and later, having collated those books and found them all in good condition - scribble-free, in fact, and sound of page and board - my own pleasure in selling them on (not to mention my profit) was also considerable.

But even today, thinking back, I have to thank the trolls who watch over booksellers, that had Mrs. Madison been less anxious to get rid of those 'dirty books', or I had been more insistent on fleeing the disappointment I'd caused her, I might have missed out on the sort of triumphant house call most booksellers only dream of.

Which still left the disposition of those two walls of unwanted books in Cavendish Crescent. They really were worthless to a bookseller, but they were certainly not worthless to readers, so I contacted Julian House, the charity that looks after homeless people in Bath, who were happy to collect them from Mrs. Madison, take them to their shop on Pulteney Bridge, and sell them at a pound or two to the reading public. All proceeds going to the maintenance of the Manvers Street night shelter. This link with Julian House was important to me, as indeed it was and is to many of my colleagues. Cherry-picking - seeking out a few valuable books from a large, mainly worthless library, paying fair money for these, but leaving the dross behind for the seller to deal with, has always made me feel a bit churlish. It's business, of course, but one can at least help (and soothe one's conscience at the same time - a bit) by getting the charity around to dispose of the unwanted books in aid of the needy. Most sellers, even faced with the stress of having to leave their homes, do understand this and are grateful for whatever help we offer. (This can also extend to putting them in touch with reliable runners or the big second-hand warehouses, both of whom may provide them with a little added cash.)

But of course there are always a few who don't understand; who feel that if I say I won't buy several hundred worthless (to me) books from them, believe I'm actually cheating them out of money they deserve: "But surely they must be worth at least £1 a book," they will insist. "There are 1000 books here, give or take, so shall we say £1000 for the lot? Or I suppose I can even make that £900, if you want to quibble."

Such blandishments are not easy to fight off - especially when there are half a dozen books among the dross that you really do want. But I have developed a certain rhetorical strategy to deal with this situation, and I shall pass it on to you now.

"The books I have chosen to buy from you," I will say, with heavily pointed patience, "come to £85. If you really want me to carry off all the others, I'm afraid I'll have to charge porterage and warehousing. That will come to about £385, so you will owe me £300. If you will therefore give me £300 now, plus the books I want, I'll see that the removals van is here at 8 a.m. tomorrow. Agreed?"

But it never is - Thank God!

******

As I said earlier, out of ignorance on both sides, one can occasionally buy books for a good deal less than they are worth; that is, for less than half what they can be resold for in the shop. But I have learned from experience that it is best not to try to correct this mistake. For example, I remember telephoning a man in a wheelchair from whom I'd bought several books on a house call to say, "It's about that book with the bright purple cover I gave you £20 for last week. Do you remember? Well, I do apologise but I've just discovered I should have given you £100. May I bring the £80 to you tomorrow?"

Silence for about half-a-minute.

"I thought you'd given a fair price for all the books you bought from me. Now you say you hadn't. Which makes me wonder if you've made other mistakes. Perhaps I should have all the books back?"

And there is no recourse - the books go back, and some other dealer makes the profit you've just thrown away by being honest and thoughtful.

Another, not dissimilar situation on house calls is the family carve-up. In this scenario, the old head of the family has just died and the new head of the family, who uses strong-smelling aftershave, wears flashy cufflinks and drives an Aston Martin, is selling Dad's library. There are three or four hundred books laid out on a large table and you have just quoted a reasonable global price for the lot. You ask if you might borrow some spare plastic bags to carry the books to your car. At which point Cufflinks says, "Oh, sorry, I promised the cousins they could choose a book or two as a souvenir of my father. Don't worry, they're all upstairs, it won't take long."

Cousin Charles surveys the books first, says he knows nothing about literature, but, well, how much is this one? Luckily he has missed the books signed by Arthur Rackham, but sadly he has chosen the *Jungle Book* first edition - so I've just said farewell to about £150 profit. In his know-nothing guise, he then picks seven more of the best books on the table, before being called off by our host so the others can have a go. It's a large extended family, and 'cousin' seems to embrace all sorts of kin. In the end I can do no more than congratulate them on their perspicacity and discrimination in selecting all the best books I'd just bought, and that yes I would be happy to give a valuation of each book. But my trade association is very insistent that members should not give free valuations and that I have to charge ten per cent of any valuation I make. (Which doesn't cover the profit I've just had to give up, but it helps a little.) In the end I still need plastic bags and the jovial cousins help me to carry them out to the car. They all seem happy with their share of the money I paid for what was left on the table. Curses!

But then, quite wonderfully heartening things can happen on house calls as well.

One morning Mr. Grayson telephoned from Bristol to suggest I might come round that evening to look at some nice flower and bird books. He mentioned Gould (wonderful elephant folio pictures of birds, equalled only by Audubon, who painted *The Birds of America*) so that evening I set off into the dusk. I usually get lost in Bristol, but Mr. Grayson's directions were excellent for someone who already knew the way. I arrived and was shown into the Book Room. The volumes housed in here were not disappointing: along with the Gould they included a long run of Curtis's *Botanical Magazine*, a publication with a frontispiece in each issue, showing a lovely hand-coloured illustration of a plant, and I enjoyed looking at each one, page by page. I told him what we could offer, and was rather disappointed when he said he would telephone the next morning with his decision. Some other dealer, I supposed, had been invited to bid as well. But I had made a fair offer, so the other dealer, if he were the lucky winner, would be over-paying.

Next day, without having telephoned, Mr. Grayson came into the shop just before lunch.

"You offered more or less the same as Jakery's. Five pounds less, actually, but you seemed to like the books better. And as you said you always get lost in Bristol, I thought I'd bring them over."

I thanked him, laid a £5 note on top of my cheque, and he said a happy goodbye to his lovely books.

After which I decided that all house calls should in future follow this script. I might even write a book about it, I thought - *The Ideal House Call* - describing in detail my dealings with Mr. Grayson.

******

In the middle of the shop, you may recall, we'd placed a tall glass cabinet meant for displaying books opened at illustrations. One morning in late Spring, a fair-haired, rather ample woman some-where well past middle age walked briskly in, crossed straight to the cabinet and took out *Eric Gill's Twenty-Five Nudes* - lovely black and white studies of a teenage girl. My first thought was - Oh, Lord - mil-itant feminist! - but that uncharitable thought was quickly dispelled when I saw the intense interest and care with which she studied each page, and I had then just decided that in fact this woman must be a teacher of art, when she turned round and with the sweetest smile said, "Of course, I was slimmer then!"

"You're Petra!" I said, startled by simple delight out of a more graceful greeting.

"I am," she laughed, came to the desk and shook hands warmly. This was Eric Gill's second daughter, the subject of those drawings, who had married Gill's co-worker at the Ditchling Community, the engraver Denis Tegetmeier, and was now living, since his death, in a beautiful converted weaving mill at Avoncliff near Bradford-on-Avon. I asked her to be kind enough to sign our Visitors' Book, which she did, and we talked about all sorts of things, most particularly her father, whose work Maryanne especially admired. Later, she asked us to tea, and pointed out that the chair I was sitting in at the head of a scrubbed table was 'where Daddy always sat'. I felt greatly honoured. Petra and Maryanne became good friends and Maryanne went to see her often over the next few years. When she died, her son asked us to look through a number of her 'Second Division books', many of which had been inscribed by Eric Gill. Maryanne bought several of them for our own library. But what I shall always remember most vividly about Petra Gill was that cheery, "Of course, I was slimmer then!" (Alas, weren't we all . . .)

I was asked by a friend of Petra's to call on Madelaine Merton who lived just outside Bath and wanted to sell her Art books. Mrs. Merton was confined to bed after a stroke and was sitting up in bed wearing a pink woollen bed-jacket when I arrived. Madelaine had been a professional artist all her life, and experience had taught me that when people are selling books which have not only been a plea-sure but have also played an influential role in their professional lives, it is not always easy to convince them that selling is the right thing to do - even though they know it is. So I was prepared to be gently sym-pathetic but firmly persuasive - if, of course, any of her books were worth buying. But Madelaine (she asked me to call her that, saying she preferred it, on the whole, to Maddy or Mad) was quite clear about selling her library: she wanted to keep only the six or seven large Herbal books on the bottom shelf, but I could have any of the others I liked.

Looking through the library, I noticed the pile of *Verve* magazines that Madelaine said would be included in the sale, and hoped one of them was the number containing the splendid double-page Matisse il-lustrations. I also noticed a long row of King Penguins, with a tell-tale book in the middle that was half an inch taller than its companions, but otherwise identical. It was, as I instantly suspected, a copy of Eric Ravilious' *High Street*, a collection of notes and lithographs depicting all the high street trades. This is generally considered to be a rare book, but Bath seemed to bristle with them, and the reason I knew what the taller book was before going near it was that people always seemed to place it in the middle of a row of King Penguins on their bookshelves. I told Madelaine this silly bit of bookseller arcana before I left that evening and it made her laugh.

I liked Madelaine a great deal and was always glad to sit by her bed and listen to her tales of Paris in the 1920's, whenever I went back to see her. On one visit she told me of a friend in Berkshire whom she really wanted to see, but the journey would be too much for her. I suggested she take a taxi and pay for it with some of the money I'd given her for her books. She felt this was a wonderful notion and began happily planning the trip - which she did make, and thoroughly enjoyed.

On another visit, I noticed that the bottom shelf where the row of Herbal books stood was empty. When I asked her about this, she said her nephew was borrowing them – he was an artist, too, and would bring them back next week after he'd made some sketches from their illustrations. I didn't say anything, but I thought, *He won't, you know* - and sure enough a few days later, I saw them for sale in an auctioneer's catalogue. I telephoned the auction house the following day and said that perhaps the collection of Herbals were being sold without the owner's permission. Oh dear, they said. But the sale went ahead and the next time I went to see Madelaine, I didn't mention the still empty bottom shelf. No point, really. She wasn't a fool, and she knew her nephew better than I did. But I still wasn't happy about it.

******

Mrs. Alban, wearing a bright pink ankle-length coat, shook her fine flaxen curls at me and declared, "I'm staying in Bath with my sister and she suggested I ask you. You see, our father died and all his books are in my house – you see, he was living with us. Anyway, he didn't have time to sort out his books and they're all just anyhow on the shelves. Golf and church architecture mainly. We're in East Sussex on the South Downs not near anywhere, I'm afraid. If you could come next Sunday morning, that would be marvellous. About ten o'clock?"

Having asked for and received slightly less Rococo directions, I set off next Sunday at half-past seven and arrived shortly after ten. The day was sunny, the South Downs sparkling, Mrs. Alban's house was as splendid as her curls. I was shown into a small, deeply carpeted room lined on every wall with books and with more books piled everywhere on the floor. My eye was caught at once by four de luxe Arthur Rackhams, with a number of other good children's books in the same pile. I asked Mrs. Alban if she wanted me to take all of them?

"As many as you like," she said. "Grandpa wanted any money

they raised to go towards little Brian's University fund."

She then said that she, little Brian and her husband (big Brian, perhaps) would be at church between 10.45 and half-past twelve, and hoped I wouldn't mind being left alone "with all this".

When they'd gone I began making piles: children's; church architecture (mostly new, with dust wrappers, including several splendid works on misericords); golf (nice, 1920's-ish books with pictures of Henry Cotton and Bobby Jones in plus fours); lots of local history (local to Brighton and Lewes, that is); and the largest pile of all – books destined for sale at the local church fête. It was now just after twelve o'clock and I began carrying books to the car. At about 12.30 the Albans and Brian reappeared and after some chat I pressed a cheque for £1150 into six-year-old Brian's hand. He inspected it carefully and passed it to Mrs. Alban who asked if I was sure, it seemed so much? I explained that the church fête could benefit from the pile left on the floor, recommended Oxford as the better university for little Brian and drove off back to Bath . . .

. . . where Maryanne and I immediately set to work cleaning and collating, polishing and pricing. Another happy ending to another typical bookseller's happy day doing house calls.

******

A nicely dressed French gentleman named Barron spent nearly an hour browsing the book shelves in the shop one morning, and then finally asked if we made the visits to houses. I said we did, and asked if he would like me to make a visit to his.

"I would, if you could be so kind," he replied. "There are many books I wish to sell, but my house is not close by - it stands twelve miles west of Chartres."

When he was younger, Nicholas had spent a good deal of time in and around Paris buying for his Notting Hill antiques shop, and when he and Victoria came down to spend the week-end with us, I asked him if he would like to act as chauffeur and guide on a driving trip to Chartres. He said of course he would. We agreed a date with

M. Barron, and two weeks later we drove to Dover, crossed the channel, drove on to Paris, garaged the car, booked rooms at the hotel Lennox in the heart of the antiques district, enjoyed a splendid meal in a restaurant near St. Germain de Pres, collected the car first thing next morning and drove down to Chartres.

M. Barron's house was in the country near Nogent-le-Rotrou, only a few minutes drive to the west of Chartres and as soon as we arrived Mme. Barron, Angele, gave us cafe au lait and brioche in the garden, and we then began looking at the books M. Barron wished to sell - some of which, a vellum bound 46-volume set of the works of Victor Hugo, for example, were certainly desirable, and many others of which, as booksellers say, were 'not quite our sort of book'. We moved from the library to the loft eventually, where Nicholas found two or three things which interested him, and in the early afternoon, we drove off with a loaded car, leaving a satisfied M. Barron by no means figuring as one of Les Miserables.

Less than a week or so after our return to Bath, a Mme Artois appeared in the shop to say that her friend Angele near Nogent-le-Rotrou had told her that we had given a fair price for her husband's books including a set of Victor Hugo's works, and could I possibly come to her house to look at some books that she wanted to sell.

"No, no, M. Bankes," she laughed, when I showed a bit of hesitation about buying more French books, "these are English books. Many of them published in the eighteenth-century which belonged to my father-in-law and no one in our town is interested in old English books. We could offer you lunch. And yes, of course, Mme. Bankes must come also!"

The following Monday, I spent another pleasant evening in Paris, this time with Maryanne, and then drove the next morning back to Nogent-le-Rotrou. We found Mme. Artois's house without difficulty and were shown straight to the books. Alas, it was not the floor-to-ceiling wall of gleaming eighteenth-century bindings we had hoped for, but two long shelves of what looked suspiciously like sermons and religious treatises.

"I hope the lunch is good," Maryanne whispered, when we'd been left alone to value our prizes.

But all was not lost. We eventually unearthed a 1683 edition of Bishop Burnet's *History of the Reformation of the Church of England* along with a number of other books which would scrub up well for those who bought by the yard. The lunch was excellent, Mme Artois was pleased that the books were not too bad, and we returned to Bath after a pleasant excursion with enough books to cover our expenses. But that was all; and as Maryanne pointed out on the ferry back to Blighty, haring about all over the continent was all well and good - and she wouldn't have missed the trip for the world - but our patch was Bath, and unless we knew in advance what we were going to find before we headed for the continent, we might do better to say 'perhaps not just now' to the good burghers of Chartres and their friends, and stick to what we felt at home with. I agreed; she was absolutely right . . .

But that lunch was awfully good.

CHAPTER EIGHT: THE COLLECTOR

"A perfectly gruesome, hairy legged…."

The collector is an altogether strange beast; but not one to be ridiculed or treated with amusement by the bookseller, as he and his fellows contribute a large proportion of the money that flows into our coffers. There are all sorts of collectors collecting all sorts of books, but the most notable and numerous among them may be categorised as: Serious; Childlike (books I loved when I was little); Family Name; Specialist (travel, architecture, cufflinks and the like); and Bindings.

The Serious Collector is so designated because he plans eventually to write the most complete bibliography ever published of a particular author. He does not know when he starts out that he will probably never finish this project. Everything is new to him, and every visit to a bookshop will be rewarding; he will invariably come away, excited as a child on his first visit to the zoo, bearing plastic bags filled with early editions of his chosen author. Soon, however, duplication will rear its frustrating head and the prizes will grow fewer and further between - at which point the serious collector, if still dedicated to his quest, will begin moving into the realms of the private edition (books produced for the author in a small, limited edition, usually paid for by himself) and the variant binding (same book, different covers).

The latter, particularly, will begin to fill the collector's mind with fearful doubts. With a large printing it is possible that the publisher, perhaps in trying to meet a deadline, will send copies of the book to two or more binders. He will give precise instructions about the colour, material, weight of boards, quantity, etc. - and will nearly always be abashed when delivery is made; for lo! the tasteful purple specified in the original order has been replaced by a garish violet! Once again, an order given in haste has resulted in disaster! The publisher gulps, hopes that the dust wrapper will hide the violet awfulness, and meets his deadline. Whew!

He has, however, left a problem for the serious collector: How many variant bindings were produced, he needs to know? For his most-complete-bibliography-ever must be painstakingly correct in this matter, and if his searches fail to unearth variant bindings other than the garish violet, he still cannot state definitively that no others exist. Like the Flying Dutchman, he begins to envisage a nightmare future for himself in which he is condemned to wander forever from bookshop to bookshop, searching for that slightly different *other* shade of purple, always hoping that the next shop or the next will at last produce it, but knowing that even if that happens there may still be yet *another* variant purple lurking out there somewhere.

For many collectors this problem may well signal abandonment of the project. For others, however, this sort of fruitless search provides a perfect excuse - (I call it the procrastinator's salvation) - not to start writing the dreaded monograph. The serious collector can then talk grandly to his friends about the definitive bibliography he will eventually write without ever having to start it because 'he is still doing some rather tricky, last-minute research.' Those last minutes can stretch on for years, and the further they stretch the greater the serious collector's reputation as a 'dedicated scholar' will become - until scholar and project together will have taken on the proportions of legend (among his friends, anyway). And when the book has at last been published (if, I should say) they will be proud to count its author as a friend. Meanwhile, the search for that shade of fugitive purple continues.

(A fugitive colour, incidentally, is defined by science as one that reacts badly to sunlight. Purple, it seems, is particularly fugitive).

******

The Child - like Collector is as vigorous in his pursuit as the serious collector, though with less scholarly motives. Nevertheless, the
collector of 'books I used to love as a child', can be as tenacious as
a bulldog - and when thwarted, just as bad-tempered. A jolly book
shop owner, when faced with such a collector, should therefore on no
account let it be known that he, along with most other bookdealers
are not very interested in children's books unless they were written by
an author who went on to write a collectable adult book, or were illustrated by a prominent illustrator, or for some other reason retained
a significant charm that persisted through the years. (*The Wind in the
Willows* is one such rare bird, *Just So Stories* another.) Bookdealers may,
and do, have their own collecting obsessions. But they are business-
men first, and if the object of someone else's obsession isn't worth
any money to them, they do have a difficult time mustering up much
interest in it, hard as they may try.

The onset of nostalgia for books one read and loved as a child
seems to appear at about age 40, and in my experience it affects men
and women with equal intensity, though it is more frequently men
who seem to succumb to the actual collecting passion. Many of the
books they seek will already have had a long reading life - books by
Enid Blyton (*The Famous Five*) or by Captain W. E. Johns (*Biggles*), for
example. Many others that were unjustly banned from school libraries, will also have secured life-long popularity among 40-plus pupils.
But if such books have no intrinsic value other than their erstwhile
popularity with children, they will certainly not maintain resale value
in the second hand market. Besides, those books have already had
one good life; the chance of them having a second outside the narrow
nostalgia market is virtually zero.

Nevertheless, avid collectors of books loved in childhood should
never be scorned or discouraged by booksellers. A grown man's
search for Inman's *The Did of Didn't-Think* is as valid to him as is the
search for signed copies of works by John Masefield to the collector of

poems about the sea. And there is always the glorious chance that in his search for Inman, the Child - like Collector may come across another old, forgotten friend. His joy then will be no less real than that of the man in search of a signed first edition of *Ulysses* who comes across a signed first edition of *The Good Soldier*. And if he has any sense, a good bookseller should join in this rejoicing, whether he understands it or not. Unexpected discoveries like that do, of course, ensure that the collector will return again and again to that same bookseller, convinced that other childhood favourites will also be found in the £2 room if he only persists. But again the good bookseller will always exercise patience and sympathy no matter how many times that ardent collector says: "I know I've asked before, but I wonder if any more books by E. S. Pirley have turned up?"

Not all collectors of children's books are motivated by nostalgia. Many, in fact, are interested only in early or first editions whose value derives uniquely from their magnificent illustrations - notably illustrations such as produced by Arthur Rackham, Edmund Dulac or Harry Clarke. The books themselves will almost always be well known children's stories such as *One Thousand and One Nights*, *Sinbad the Sailor*, and *Tales of the Brothers Grimm*. The illustrators of the early 1900's like Rackham, Dulac and Clarke have held children spellbound for over a century now, and first editions of their works, bound in vellum and signed by the artist, with each illustration protected by its own fly leaf, are regularly offered at auction for over £1000 each. Of course a price like this assumes that the book is immaculate: elegant colouring in a child's hand adds nothing to the value of a book already coloured by a famous illustrator, though children in possession of crayons rarely seem to grasp this fact.

Collecting books published since WWII which are illustrated by modern artists is, as with any modern book, more of a gamble. For such collectors, it is useful to remember that if the first edition of any children's book is published in large numbers (the first *Harry Potter*, for example was printed in the hundreds of thousands of copies, so strong was the advance promotion), those books will have no rarity value at all, and may not begin commanding interesting prices at auction for decades. People have frequently brought me copies of the first

Harry Potter and waited in breathless anticipation for my valuation. "I'm sorry," I am always obliged to say, "I haven't looked through it yet, but if this copy is still in pristine condition then it is presently worth a few pence less than what you paid for it. If not, it's worth very little, I'm afraid."

Nevertheless, a good collection can be made of fine copies of current children's favourites. Their popularity may have waned in the playground, but such classics as Roald Dahl's subversive horror stories illustrated by Quentin Blake have been rightly popular for long enough to have built up a strong future nostalgia market. When dealing with modern books for children, the collector can follow his own taste and can combine the pleasure of collecting with the delight of watching his own predilection appreciate in value. Choosing hitherto unrecognised children's books means, of course, reading them in order to select promising authors and illustrators. If seen doing this on lunch breaks at work, the practice may earn one some rather odd looks from office colleagues and may even damage one's promotion prospects - but the only way to judge which children's books may be collectable in future is to read them, and if being seen doing this earns public scorn, so be it. Obsession is all in collecting.

The availability of Mint, Fine or Very Good quality children's books that may tempt collectors is a constant problem for booksellers - not just because children's books are so often mistreated but because they are so often thrown away after the child they were written for has grown up a bit. For a year or two after publication, though, Fine copies do tend to be available. But remember, the description 'Fine' means without any defect, and the constant handling of books, especially by children, can easily lead to chips at the top and bottom edges of dust wrappers - a defect of no importance to the book's artistic merit but one which seriously affects price in the collector's realm. A chip to the dust wrapper can mean instant downgrading to 'Very Good' or, at best, 'Fine, but small chip to top edge of dust wrapper'. And if dealer and collector, or two dealers, are trading online, an inaccurate description means that a book purchased for a considerable sum can be returned and money refunded without question. Postage must sometimes also be refunded. Accurate descriptions are therefore essential to any book sale, particularly a children's book, that is not conducted face to face. A collector should also confine his buying exclusively to books accurately described as 'Mint', 'Fine', or 'Very Good'. If the description is merely 'Good' it may refer to a severely defective book, while the term 'Reading Copy' may well describe a spavined, broken-backed thing, smelling strongly of smoke, which only the most devoted lover of that author would even agree to hold.

Finally, among the Child - like Collectors, there are a number of children who collect children's books. But there is also a rare subgenre called 'children who collect books that are not children's books'. Michael Ford, an after-school habitué of Bankes Books, was one such; a fourteen-year-old arachnophile (the opposite of arachnophobe, I suppose) who was a passionate collector of books about spiders. Smiling was not Michael's strong suit - but I watched his face light up one afternoon when he found, in an illustrated encyclopaedia of the insect world, a magnificent double-page photograph of a perfectly gruesome, hairy-legged tarantula – one that would have sent Miss Muffett screaming down Margarets Buildings for her life. He told me that originally he had wanted to collect butterfly books, but the first one that took his fancy was the standard work by Humphreys and Westwood that cost £250. He'd thought of saving up for it, but didn't think he'd live long enough, so he switched to spiders. (I didn't argue the logic with him.) The tarantula, he said, would be the prize of his collection, and he would carefully remove the illustration and pin it up on his bedroom wall - (which would, I feared, cause his mother to do her own Miss Muffet, though again I refrained from comment).

Some days later, I found another terrifying tarantula picture in a bundle of pages torn from an eighteenth century natural history work. I placed this in the front window, thinking young Michael would be pleased to see it there on his way home from school and perhaps even decide to add it to his collection. But before he even had a chance to see it, a rather forceful woman, with a ruddy complexion and a pearl necklace, hurried into the shop and asked if she could look more closely at the spider in the window. Not my idea of a sensible thing to do, but business is business, so I crawled into the window space, retrieved the horrible illustration - (wondering as

I risked dislocation doing it, if I should also capture the real spider in the corner and present that to her as a bonus) - only to hear behind me as I backed out with whatever dignity I could muster.

"It's for my son, Michael, you see. He's crazy about spiders. Do you think that's quite healthy?"

So mother *had* seen and survived the double-page monster, this new spider would now be joining it on Michael's wall, and therefore all was well in the eight-legged world of the Ford family.

As for 'quite healthy', I declined yet again to offer an opinion.

******

The Family Name Collector falls into much the same category as the 'books I used to love as a child' collector. He is also determined and seeks with optimism a book written by a great-grandfather, all known copies of which have long since been pulped. Again, this fate is best not disclosed to him by the bookseller. Such a book may indeed turn up, and anyway the book next to *Bojangles* in the £2 room may have some interest for *Mr. Bojangles* and he may wish to add it to his slim collection.

One such Family Name Collector of far greater interest came in one day. She was very attractive and asked whether I had any unusual editions of *Alice in Wonderland*. This is not an uncommon request, and I was glad to be able to show her one written in shorthand and another translated into Danish. She bought them both, and I was startled to find that she had signed the cheque Alice Liddell.

"Can this be right?" I asked, and she explained that she was indeed related to the Dean of Christ Church who had written the original *Alice*. I explained then that it was a house rule to write cheque card numbers on all cheques, and was relieved that the name on the card was indeed Alice Liddell and not Mrs. Charles Chaplin. She left her address and telephone number and asked me to look out for other unusual copies. I was very glad to do so, though I never came up with another as curious as Alice written in shorthand.

Another Family Name collector was William Thackeray. I didn't like to ask if his middle name was Makepeace, but it seemed to make no difference. He was short, tubby and wore very strong spectacles. I asked him if he was interested only in first editions, and he said no, he was a voracious collector and liked to give copies of books by Thackeray, the elder, to people who came to stay with him or (if he had particularly enjoyed the occasion) to those who came to dine. On the whole, he admitted, he preferred to buy less expensive copies of works by his illustrious ancestor. Late editions of *Vanity Fair*, he said, were not hard to find, of course but - fighting off a simper - he did tend to entertain a great deal. I supposed that many of his guests recycled their 'dining presents' at Christmas time, and was glad to think that the works of the great man were still thus in circulation.

It may be that a member of the collector's family was a book-binder, and signed his work with a tiny printing in gilt of his name. This signature might be found on the upper board binding, or on the lowest fold-over, but sometimes also appears on the lower board and, less frequently, in black at the top of a free fly leaf. The search for such a signed binder will give the collector an excellent reason to go through every leather-bound book in the shop, perhaps dropping one or two in the process. If this happens, the bookdealer may consider himself justified in using the forbidden phrase: "Oh, Dashwood? Let me see. Yes, I believe we had one yesterday. Sorry."

******

For three successive Saturday mornings, the shop was visited by a short, fit-looking man in his 70's wearing a brown tweed jacket, cavalry twill trousers and the same bright red tie. On the second and third visits he marched to the row of A & C Black books and pulled down only one of the other twenty or so on the shelf - the one about the Durbar, with pictures of the Indian army officers in their fine red, green and blue uniforms. *Annals of Skinner's Horse* was not, as some might have thought, a companion volume to *Black Beauty*. It was, however, exactly the sort of book sought after by Major Garton-Green, a serious collector of books about the Indian army, including the army of the East India Company. The Indian army wore colourful and exciting uniforms, and the A & C Black volume devoted to the Durbar of the early 1900's is one of the most handsome books of that popular series. Major Garton-Green had been a soldier in the Indian army and told me, as he stood, straight-backed and with waxed moustache in front of my desk, that the biggest crime of both the First and Second World Wars had been the blind disruption of the proud Indian regiments. The finest troops in the world, he said, were murdered in the trenches. He admitted that what really grieved him was the disdain of officers of the British army for officers of the Indian army.

"Almost as if we, ourselves, were native, by God," he asserted in deep political incorrectness - which incorrectness, had he acknowledged it, would not have bothered him one iota.

The major visited the shop on a number of occasions and as the years passed I noticed with sadness that his proud spruceness was sinking down the lane to seediness. One afternoon he asked me gruffly if I'd care to come to tea. I must have shown some surprise – he had never suggested this before – and, his voice almost strangled with embarrassment, he said, "Got to sell a few things. Short commons, y' know."

On an afternoon in May, when William was looking after the shop, I drove to the village of Doynton outside Bath, where Mrs. Garton-Green opened the door. She was as short as her husband and seemed strangely frightened to see me there. She showed me into the sitting room and offered me tea, China or Assam. I chose Assam and the major, who was standing at the fireplace, hands clasped behind back, seemed pleased at this, and told me of a holiday they had spent in Assam, "Best holiday for the fisher fleet. Cools them down."

He grinned at his wife who, now less frightened, smiled back. (I knew that the so-called 'fisher fleet' were in fact the English women who, armed with a number of photographs of themselves on thick card, sailed to India in search of husbands. They were always met at the docks by an eager crowd of army officers who seized a copy of the photograph, scribbled name and rank on the back, and returned to their barracks to dream of a potential wife. For just as the ladies needed to be married, so the officers were in search of a wife. The rule was originally 'majors and above', but so many wives died of India's plagues and fevers that the rule was relaxed and feminine company was extended to 'wives of captains and above').

Major Garton-Green then asked his wife to "leave the men to business, my dear" and invited me to look through the books, a number of which had come from Bankes Books some years before. I tried to advise him that he might do better if he asked me to sell them in the shop, keeping a small commission on each, but he was insistent that there was no time for this. I think the discipline of the mess bill had cast a shadow. I stretched my estimates to an upper level and wrote him a cheque for £2765, explaining that I would get back a bit more than twice this. He clutched the cheque and calling to his wife, waved it in front of her. "There!" he announced, almost gleefully. "Told you the Army wouldn't let me down."

******

Specialist Collectors, in my experience, are nothing if not special. To wit: one afternoon, I was thoughtfully polishing a hungry full calf book, when I became aware of someone standing at the side of my desk. I looked up and smiled. (Never say, "Can I help you?" as this tends to frighten.) He was dressed in a black jacket, black waistcoat, and striped trousers. His dark hair was oiled and parted down the middle, and he wore a silver goatee like the rich uncle in a 1930's Fred Astaire film. He gave the impression of being exactly the sort of person he liked to be, and confirmed this with a wide, white smile.

This was, in fact, Mr. Weatlake, whose collecting passion was focused upon what he called 'dancing books'. When he first asked for these, I produced several coffee-table ballet books and a fat, rather solemn tome on the history of dance. With great sadness, worthy of any 1930's film extra, he pushed these aside, as if he had been shown such things so many times before that the very sight of them wearied him unto the grave.

"There are two or three Victor Sylvester books downstairs in the £2 room," I tried. At which, to my amazement, his eyes lit up and he soft-shoed deftly across the room to the stairs. Ten minutes later he re-emerged with, in fact, four Sylvester books and a bright, triumphant smile. He became a regular visitor and whenever something that interested him turned up he would buy it. Though in fact I never did quite grasp what he meant by 'a collectable dancing book'.

William had previously spent some time on the staff of the Economic Intelligence Unit, and when I discovered by accident that one of my regular customers, Andrew Baring, had also acted for them, I invited them both to lunch at one of the restaurants in Margarets Buildings. They got on famously from the start, and have, I believe, remained friends to this day. So I look on that lunch as another good deed done.

In one or other of his many visits to the shop, Andrew had told me that he'd lived with his mother in Bradford-on-Avon, and continued to do so after her death. He made it clear that he was intensely proud of being a Baring and thus related to Sir Evelyn Baring, 1st Earl of Cromer and former British Controller-General in Egypt. I formed the impression that the family connection was rather more tenuous than he was letting on, and that when the time came to draw up lists of those to be invited to weddings, his name did not spring naturally from the pen. But this did not get in the way of his enthusiasm for the family name, or for his determination, he told me, to build the most complete possible collection of books about West Africa that he could afford.

Andrew had been born in West Africa and already had a very large number of books about the area. In addition, he was aiming to amass a complete collection of the little *Oxford World's Classics* and first came to the shop because I had once filled a small bookcase in the window with them. I remember he'd spent about twenty minutes checking my books against his master list. He found fourteen he didn't have and we agreed on a reasonable price. In discussing the books, he solved a mystery for me. Four or five of the titles were by a lady novelist, whose name appeared in this series but was otherwise unknown. Andrew told me that the Editor-in-Chief of the series was wildly in love with that lady novelist and, against the advice of all his colleagues at OUP, had insisted on publishing her books.

******

Bindings Collectors are not interested in the titles of the books they collect, the names of their authors, their publishers, their illustrators, their editors, their typography designers or the men or women who wrote their introductions. Their shelves at home only hold books that have been bound by a particular bindery: Sangorski & Sutcliffe, for example, or Rivière, and they will spend much time in a bookshop opening the upper covers of every leather-bound book searching for the binder's mark. Or bindings may be amassed randomly for the artistic fineness of the work alone. Or they may, for example, be eighteenth century French bindings, or the wooden bindings of incunabula (those printed before 1400). The limits set for themselves by collectors of this kind are as varied as the collectors themselves. But funds play a most important role in collections based on aesthetic criteria since books of this kind may well be the most expensive ever published.

Maryanne's family were for many generations determined book collectors on a par with Beckford or Gibbon. When we were first engaged, Maryanne asked if I would catalogue the books in the library at Winstanley, the house where her family had lived for over five hundred years. The library was a large room lined with adjustable shelves. Each shelf was laden with books weighed down by the accumulated dust of a hundred years or so. The house had been requisitioned by the RAF in the war, and in the succeeding years thieves had stripped the roof of most of its lead, so damp drove the family to living downstairs. Luckily the library escaped the damage. I was given some library stairs, a pen and a large notebook, and gradually began to discover which members of the family collected what sort of books. In the eighteenth-century, for example, three successive generations of Bankes's bought thrilling books of sermons and other religious works.

I also came to the conclusion that every keeper of the library after about 1700 had used the same bookbinder, and as I clambered about on my library ladder making notes in my notebook, I began to imagine myself as a London bookseller faithfully fulfilling a standing order for Mr. Bankes of Winstanley: "The latest book of sermons, please, to be bound in the usual style of full calf with Cambridge panels."

To my regret, I discovered that none of the nineteenth-century Bankes family, despite the example of their progenitor Joseph Bankes, seemed to have had any interest at all in travel - though I did find a reference in an earlier keeper's listing to Captain George Vancouver's circumnavigation, 'including the atlas'. The book had been lent to a friend living in a nearby great house. She was obviously of a knowledgeable and discriminating nature because the book had never been returned. The atlas volume had gone missing, too - more knowledge and discernment, presumably. But some 40 years later, while attending auctions in London I saw the atlas listed in one sale and the other Vancouver volumes in another. All the volumes and the atlas were described as bearing the Bankes bookplate, so I bought them at slightly over the estimates, was delighted that my friend Michael Smith subsequently bought them from me, and I am now happy to know that they are safely gracing his shelves.

The Bankes family stopped collecting books during the war, but until then had built up a famous collection of sporting books. The hunting volumes, after the long debates in Parliament about banning the sport, rather surprisingly retained their popularity, though the subject of hunting, itself, was usually broached with preliminary coughs and a certain amount of near neighing. Fishing books are always popular and there is somehow such a respect for the sport that books about coarse fishing or angling are nearly always attractively produced.

Shooting books are a little less popular. But one of the great collectors of shooting books was Chris Cradock, coach to the British team, who, once he became aware of my own interest in the sport, would recommend Bankes Books to other shooters. He told me he particularly enjoyed his Christmas present from Bankes Books which took a liquid form; good, he said, for steadying the hand.

Sometimes a binding collector will be looking specifically for the prize bindings awarded by a particular school - perhaps hoping to find an award won by a grandfather long ago. I was puzzled one afternoon in the shop when a man I had taken for a 'birthday' shopper took a tape measure out of his pocket and began measuring half a dozen or so duodecimo books. Was this a new thieves' ploy? Were the little books going to be cunningly transferred to pockets under pretence of being measured? Or was it a question of having a book-case with very squat shelves - no room for anything taller than duo-decimo? My puzzled close attention must eventually have made the puzzle-setter feel nervous enough to offer an explanation - which was that he wanted to 'mould' them (mould them?) and therefore they needed to be exactly the same height and have perfect spines. I feared this might be a preamble to a request to borrow the books, but there seemed to be no question of that, and money changed hands for an attractive amount. A month or so later he was looking for more iden-tical bindings, this time tall octavo. As he paid, he placed on the desk a beautiful little pencil-holder made from the spines of the books he had bought from me. "For you, Mr. Bankes," he smiled, and left. *Of course, a mould - I knew it all along.*

*****

Most collectors start collecting books already familiar to them. These might be about a part of the world where they frequently travel; or an artist they admire; or a particular genre of crime novel (Simenon and Christie are both great favourites - as of course are, Conan Doyle and Poe). But probably the most popular of all the fields of collection is modern first editions. Collecting and dealing in modern first editions is, as all booksellers know, treading in one of the most volatile of all market places. The first hurdle is to establish 'what is modern?'

There is no agreed-upon answer to this, but books generally re-garded as modern by dealers are those published 50 years ago or less. Notable exceptions will be James Bond novels, which proudly stand on the shelves of most Modern Firsts collectors. The first edition of Ian Fleming's first Bond book, *Casino Royale*, is especially desirable - largely because of its relative rarity. When a publisher is considering how many copies to print of a hitherto unpublished author he will, unless the appearance of the book is accompanied by *Harry Potter*-like clamour, risk printing only a thousand or two copies. This will not be because of any uncertainty on his part – he knows that his own judgment is unimpeachable – but alas, he cannot rely on potential readers to display the same degree of good judgement. If the first printing sells out, however, it takes only days to produce a second printing of, perhaps, six thousand copies. The history of his lucubrations will be shown on the back of the page which shows the title, author, publisher and date of the current edition. This page is called the Title Page and the back of it is the verso. So the verso of the title page shows the date of each printing until the current edition. It may also show one of the arcane numerals which coding experts will decipher as 0 to 10, in numerical order. At each printing the last print number will be omitted. This is known as the drop-off number, and is useful in establishing the 'true first' of a book, though not the number of copies printed. If, as is common, the only line of printing information on the verso of the title page reads 'First published 2012', collectors new to the field may mistakenly believe that this implies the existence of an earlier edition. This is not so: the last line of information refers to the current edition and if there is only one line, then the collector is indeed looking at a first edition. In any event, it is one of those one or two thousand copies of *Casino Royale* that modern first collectors are looking for, and they are as rare as a plain heroine in a 007 film.

If you watch an experienced dealer examining a book, you will see him looking at its bottom edge; not the lower board, but the bottom edge. He is looking for a mark, a single stripe made, for example, by a felt pen. Such a mark will have been made by a bookseller on the discovery of a fault such as a missing page, a page creased during binding, a marked page, or even a book smelling of smoke and perhaps rescued from a fire. The wise modern first collector will take note of this mark and look for the fault it denotes before committing money.

An unpleasant habit amongst the pond life dealing in first editions is that known as 'making up'. A dealer may have come by a good copy of a valuable book which sadly has a missing plate. The dealer will keep this copy safe until he comes across a poor copy of the book which however has a good copy of the plate in question. He will make up his good copy with the good page from the poor copy, using an effective non-acid glue, and lo and behold he has a valuable book for sale, perfect in every way. Except that it isn't.

Another reason for describing this 'modern first' venture as a gamble is the fashion element. A not very good book may be fashionable as the result of an accompanying film, or because of the prestige of the author (though political memoirs may usually be excluded - the memoirs of a popular politician may be printed in large numbers and thus have no rarity value, while those of a politician not widely known are likely to be dull unless the author was close to power and likes to peddle gossip). One-day-wonders are of value only when the book was published before the wonderful event occurred. *My Life As a Ship's Chandler* by Joe Marston was printed with low expectations as far as numbers were concerned until Joe Marston cut up his wife and posted bits of her body to fictitious addresses all over the world. Then every collector wanted a first edition of this wonderful man's book!

Signed copies of modern firsts may decrease the value of a nice clean copy, though if the author was not particularly interesting in the first place, it will only be decreasing a low-value book. A book signed by gruesome Joe Marston will maintain its value. There is something compelling about an author's signature which adds to the immediacy of any book, modern first or not, and sometimes the signature of a friend – or better yet, an enemy – of the author can add value. Such a signature converts a book into what is termed an 'association copy'.

For instance, an early copy of Joe's book inscribed to his wife Marleen on the title page and with her signature on the front free pastedown page might have a gruesome attraction. Apart from such literary gems, however, uninteresting signatures do not add value to modern firsts that are already interesting.

Bookshop owners will often meet another type of modern first: a book which has sunk without trace into a deep, black publishing pool, and is wanted now only by its own author. His favourite pastime, according to his wife, is 'browsing in second-hand bookshops'.

Loyalty prevents her from adding, 'looking for copies of his book', but this is the sad truth. He has given away the half-dozen free copies allotted to him by his publisher; he has given away the dozen copies he bought himself hoping that those sales might boost his chances

of making the best-seller list, and now, encouraged by the ready conversations about his book wherever he goes, he is determined to satisfy local demand by keeping his promise to 'send a copy, do'. They
don't mean it, of course. They only feel sorry for him because nobody
liked his book. But he doesn't know that. And if someone told him
he wouldn't believe it. So on he goes, forever on the lookout for a
second-hand bookshop that has that elusive copy that he can send to
one of his fans.

And who knows - one day someone with clout in the publishing
world may stumble across that unloved book, look at it, and say, 'Hold
on, this is great!' It does happen, you know.

******

George Hempstead used to burst into the shop about once every
three months carrying his motor-bike helmet under his arm, bloated
with bulky biking clothes, smiling cheerily and asking for books about
windmills. And every time he appeared I would have to say 'Sorry'
and shake my head no, and out he'd go again looking sad. After about
a year he told me he thought he must now have secured all the books
there were about windmills and had now decided to start collecting
books about treen - little objects made of wood, such as snuff boxes
and shoe-horns. The next time he came in I showed him a wooden
board, about the size of a bagatelle board I'd just acquired in a junk
shop. It had about forty little wooden protuberances and a Victorian
label on the back explaining that it was for reading and writing for the
blind. George bought it at once, saying it was the largest thing in his
new collection, but what he'd actually come in for were books about
treen, not treen itself - what would I sell him next, a sandpit?

I accepted his rebuke meekly, and explained that I had bought
the thing only that morning, intending to do some research on what I
took to be a pre-Braille invention.

After George left I began thinking of all the different treen objects
I had seen in my life —combs for currying horses, toadstools for darn-
ing socks, little wedges for holding cupboard doors open, or keeping
them shut, cribbage pegs - beautiful, hand-carved cribbage pegs . . .

Good Lord, I was thinking just like a collector! I moved from treen to books on fencing, then books with a Churchill connection, always terribly expensive, and with most signatures forgeries. Another golden vein of mine consisted of books about Bath, from the eighteenth to the twenty first-century. These included the satirical *Minuet of Bath* which stretched across the whole of the shop window, briefly causing much interest before it sold very quickly for £2000.

In the end I began to see that almost anything could form the basis of a collection, books with flawed illustrations, books about shoes, or sheep, or spectacles, or surgical instruments. The eye of the collector never blinks!

Shopkeepers, of course, must never be tempted to become collectors themselves. Shop keeping is about making a profit, and this most laudable of all aims, will be instantly rendered null if even a single book one can sell today for £20 is hidden away in a Back Room with the excuse that it may be worth £30 in a year or two.

In their vigorous search for books of a particular kind and quality, it is sometimes hard to distinguish between a collector and a dealer. But a dealer is a dealer is a dealer - and he must remain that however tempting the temptation to do otherwise may be!

CHAPTER NINE: DEALING

Lexicon hit!

It is, of course, un-British to bargain or haggle about the price of anything. Nevertheless, a successful bookshop owner must be adept at recognising which customers expect a discount, and which will actually deserve one. Nearly everybody likes to feel they have secured a bargain, and since the experienced dealer has certainly priced his books so that he can afford to give a fellow dealer a ten per cent discount, it should be no hardship to offer the same discount to a deserving customer. Even better, the bookseller is in a unique position to offer that discount without subjecting the customer to the indignity of having to ask for it. As a book priced at £50, say, is being wrapped, the dealer can simply say, "I think we might manage £45 for this."

The result will be a pleasant one for both - though it does violate the age-old law that at the conclusion of any bargaining, both parties should feel slightly dissatisfied. (This law, incidentally, is regularly mis-interpreted as suggesting that both parties should feel they have won; when what it suggests, in fact, is that one party has won too much.) Be that as it may, the graceful offer of a discount without resorting to vulgar haggling, is the first rule of dealing to be followed by any bookshop owner who wants to have a happy life and lots of returning customers.

The second rule for dealing, much practised in the souk but often neglected in the bookshop, is always to know in advance exactly what price you are prepared to pay/accept for any book. If you do not have this figure clearly in mind, the buyer/seller will detect the weakness instantly and such pointed remarks as, "Couldn't you make it a bit less/more?" will have to be met with an obdurate, "I'm afraid not." Supplemental to this rule of 'knowing your price' is always to start off a bit higher/lower so that you can give/take a little during the bargaining process (in the souk this is known as 'prepared to sell for ten, but asking first for a thousand').

Once these basic rules have been mastered the serious student-bookseller can begin to absorb the subsidiary rules - beginning with book-buying: People will often bring into the shop a "valuable" book and ask the proprietor what it is worth. It is important at this opening stage to make clear that the fee for valuing any book will be ten per cent of the value given; said fee being of course waived if the book is then offered for sale to the bookseller at that price. It was my habit when doing a valuation always to explain, as well, that I would only offer to buy the book for half of what I expected to sell it for, and that the vendor was free to come into the shop at any time to see what price I had marked on the flyleaf.

Occasionally people queried what they saw as a frankly greedy hundred per cent profit being made from their precious book. I would patiently explain that some of that profit went on rent and rates, some on utility bills, some on my breakfast, some on William Burman's wages, some on the monthly rental of the obligatory burglar alarm, some on the length of time a book remained on the shelf - and that in the end, when all of that was factored in, my profit actually worked out at about ten per cent. Some were mollified, some weren't. The Mollified would say, 'Yes, I do see,' or merely, 'Oh, dear'; the Weren'ts would say, 'You think I don't have to pay the gas bill, too?'

The plastic bags that came through the door of Bankes Books often contained Bibles or Prayer Books; no one likes to throw these away, and very often they remain sadly in good condition, but, because they are so common they are rarely worth much. The same applies to Special Coronation Numbers of newspapers, always carefully stored away in the sock drawer along with Grandpa's note saying, 'This will be worth a lot some day!' optimistically paper-clipped to the top edge. The paper-clip has rusted, destroying what little value the Souvenir Edition ever had, but the optimism remains and the treasure will be carried from shop to shop before it dawns on the owner that the booksellers are not working in concert to cheat them and, (sigh), perhaps they do know more about the souvenir edition market than Grandpa did.

Even so, states the next supplementary rule: do not denigrate this unsaleable offering. Comment favourably on its well-preserved colour, its lack of extra creases, its freedom from tears and foxing. And do not, above all, tell the disappointed vendor that this is the fifth such piece of rubbish you have had to refuse today. Why? Because this disappointed vendor will remember how nice you were to them, and may one day return with another treasure preserved on Grandpa's silly advice - only this time it may be a first edition of Winnie the Pooh signed by the author and dedicated to Grandpa, himself, whom the vendor neglected to mention was H.G. Wells.

******

The popular image of an antiquarian bookdealer is very much flawed. It is the image of a remarkably lazy, overweight windbag who drinks far too much port, eats far too many oysters, and then very occasionally, feeling the need to re-finance their mode de vie, steps outside the front door, hand outstretched and is immediately rewarded with wads of £50 notes thrust forward by legions of fawning bibliophiles . . .

Please do not be deceived. That figure does not represent our kind. One evening in Spring, when I was still trading at the Wednesday Market, Charles Russell, my erstwhile son-in-law, telephoned to ask if I would like to join him the next day on a book-buying run. I said I would like that very much and as I climbed into his car at dawn the next day he handed me a list of the six bookshops we would be visiting that morning (all in Surrey or Hampshire), and the eight we'd being going to in the afternoon.

Whizzing along the leafy lanes of Hampshire, I asked him what, from his point of view, was the most important thing about the first bookshop we'd be visiting.

"That there is easy parking," he said, not making a joke. "I don't like being towed away and I don't like paying fines to get out of pounds. And if the bookshop with the good parking is near two or three others, so much the better. As for what's on offer inside, if they have books I can profit from, that's a great shop. If they don't, it's rubbish."

We stormed from shop to shop, spending what seemed to me quite a leisurely time in each, but in fact getting through all six on the morning list at breakneck-speed. Charles clearly had a friendly relationship with each bookseller he introduced me to, and not one of them seemed anything other than delighted to see him. When I remarked on this he gave me a very serious look.

"I never just put my head round the door and say, 'Anything for me?' the way I did when I started out", he explained, as we crossed from Hampshire into Sussex. "The next shop we're visiting is in Petersfield. It's where I learned my lesson about that. A few years ago, I stopped in, shoved my head round the door, asked if they had anything for me, and the owner said, 'Yes,' and threw a Greek Lexicon at me. Nearly took my eye out. Now I always take the time to say hello at every shop, chat a bit, and look carefully at the books I specialise in. This only takes a few minutes and the bookseller feels you're paying him the compliment of supposing he's acquired something new and interesting since you were last in. When the shop is empty, he may even suggest there might be something in the Back Room, and he will conduct you there as if you were Aladdin who had just had a good rub of the lamp."

******

That was a lesson in diplomatic courtesy which never failed me and for which I shall always be thankful to Charles. Another lesson, involving more practical matters, nearly sent Bankes Books spiralling into bankruptcy, and taught me the real value of that tired old homily: If you want it done right, *don't* do it yourself.

About a year after we'd opened, two charming gentlemen from Hong Kong came into the shop and began looking seriously at a great range of books. They proceeded slowly from shelf to shelf, consulting as they went, every so often returning to lay the books they'd chosen in a neat pile on my desk. After perhaps an hour of this, the piles had grown quite tall, and the gentlemen asked me politely how much all the books would cost: "Your price to include postage, please," they requested.

I hadn't the faintest idea how much it would cost to send 125 books to Hong Kong - so I said so, and asked the gentleman who had made the request what he thought. Smiling broadly he named a figure for the postage to Hong Kong. Smiling just as broadly, I doubled it and added it to the combined prices of all the books they'd bought when I'd finished totting them up. I gave them that figure as the sale price and awaited their response, certain that I'd left myself plenty of margin for the round of bargaining I assumed would now begin. (I'd spent a year in Malaysia and knew that the Chinese enjoy bargaining almost as much as gambling, which comes second only to educating their children.) In fact, they both seemed to think the figure I'd quoted was perfectly fair, and the deal was done almost before I realised it.

That afternoon, when I'd finally staggered down to the Post Office after an hour doing battle with a lot of brown paper and sellotape, I was astonished to discover that the price of postage for those 125 books was roughly double the figure I'd arrived at after doubling their original estimate. I was told, in fact, that for that number of books it would be cheaper to use an international courier service. Which I duly did - not happily, but duly - and thereby rescued a morsel of profit from what I'd been telling myself earlier was a most substantial sale.

A word to the novice dealer therefore: When a question of cost involving anything as arcane as postal rates arises, don't trust a customer's opinion, or your own, or your spouse's, or that of anybody else who happens to be within hailing distance. Get yourself some scales and a sheet of Post Office rates!

******

It is good to remember, too, that books which seem common-place to an English bookseller may appear fresh and exciting to a foreign dealer. For example, an American dealer who specialised in architectural history came into the shop one day and was delighted to find in the downstairs room a whole shelf-full of tedious architecture texts and out-of-date Bannister Fletchers that I'd bought for peanuts from a local professor of design who had retired and was moving to a smaller house. I'd expected to make £20 from the lot - if I were lucky - but the American dealer was perfectly happy to pay the £5 I asked for each one, and even confessed after he'd written the cheque that he almost felt guilty for having done so well out of the deal at my expense. I refrained from replying that value, like beauty, lies in the eye of the beholder. Nor did I confess that I'd never have made anything like that much from an English dealer.

What pleased me most, though, was that I'd never treated those books as anything other than interesting bargain basement stock. If I'd immediately marked them up and displayed them importantly in the expectation of the arrival of an American dealer in architectural history, that dealer would never have appeared - until, of course, after years of looking at the wretched things staring mournfully back at me from their prominent shelves, I'd finally slashed the prices and moved them to the basement. *Then* within 48 hours, two or three American dealers would have appeared, all clamouring for just such books. And I'd keep thinking forever after: *If only I'd waited a little bit longer.* No self-respecting bookdealer wants to suffer regrets like that - there's no profit in it - or fun.

And while I'm on the subject of American bookdealers . . .

The first time Mr. Norgard entered the shop it was as if a whirl-wind had come to see us. He arrived with four lieutenants and they tackled their task with military precision. Each was despatched to one quarter of the shop and every book in stock was picked up and examined. It made me suspect that Mr. Norgard must once have missed an epic bargain in a bookshop somewhere in Europe, and the sadistic dealer who'd found that bargain later, went out of his way to tell him what he'd missed.

Following his forensic examination of my stock, Mr. Norgard informed me that he had a large, second-hand bookshop in Idaho, and that he restricted the books on his shelves to 'strictly clean and saleable'. He was a tall, powerful man whose chest seemed to be built for rows of medals. Breathing heavily, he sat down by my desk and asked if I had anything especially nice? 'Any Conan Doyle? Any Mark Twain?' I reached onto the shelf behind me and handed him my first edition copy of Twain's *The Celebrated Jumping Frog of Calaveras County*. This was Mr. Clemens' first published short story, I explained, and Mr. Norgard looked as if he wanted to leap up with a glad cry when he took the handsome little book in his hands. Instead, with commendable calm, he immediately offered me twice the marked price and, with equally commendable calm, I accepted. For the next ten minutes, while Mr. Norgard told me how important he was 'book-dealer-wise' in the Idaho-Washington-Oregon area, the lieutenants returned to my desk one by one and each laid a pile of books before their captain. He acknowledged each offering with a small nod, and he did appear to be pleased, but he also seemed to imply that, yes, such books were certainly fine, but that without running about all over the shop, he, Mr. Norgard, had discovered a first edition of *The Jumping Frog*. Having made that announcement, he then invited the lieutenants to lunch 'on him' and asked me where the nearest really good restaurant was. I recommended the Royal Crescent Hotel. I reckoned the lieutenants deserved a bit of a treat.

******

Elizabeth Hutcheons, seventy-ish in a once fashionable black suit, came into the shop three times without buying anything. Then on her fourth visit she delved into a large bag and pulled out half a dozen First World War trench maps. These are always interesting, and especially so if, as these did, they showed trenches in an infamous battle zone like Ypres. She also produced several mud-stained issues of the *Wipers Times* and then asked, with great dignity, if I might buy such articles as these. After I'd assured her I did buy such articles, we talked briefly about her father, whom she'd obviously adored, and she told me how he had returned from France, slightly wounded, but often speaking of how every man in his platoon had died. I looked more closely at the maps and saw at one corner, written in ink, the instruction: 'Eastings before Northings'. Which was quite different from the usual notation for reading map references, and I wondered suddenly if Captain Hutcheons had made the note himself, and if this might be the cause of his having lost his entire platoon. There seemed little to be gained by explaining this anomaly to Miss Hutcheons, who was clearly facing financial difficulties with as much courage as her father had faced the Hun.

I paid her a generous price for these sad memories of her father - who must have looked, I thought after she'd left, terribly dashing in his Sam Browne belt - and sounded terribly unreliable muttering, "Eastings first, then Northings, oh dash it, Northings before Eastings. I shan't ever get it right. Better jot it down here . . . "

******

My experience in the bookshop taught me that the most skilful of all European dealers were the Italians. Several of them visited Bankes Books every two or three months and all seemed to have been trained at the Buy Cheaply College of Bargaining. They would find a book and check the plates carefully, then launch a sustained charm attack, interspersed with:

"You agree, then."

"Special price, very special price."

"I think we can make a small reduction, yes?"

"I buy many books here, you give me favoured customer rate, yes?"

All this with quick, distracting hand movements, almost touching me, and done with a huge smile as if it was all a game. Which of course it was – played for money by an expert.

Paolo Ventori always telephoned a week or so before he came

in. Like the other two Italian dealers who visited us regularly, Paolo was looking for books which featured views of Italy. He didn't particularly enjoy the hunt for such books, but threw himself with enthusiasm into the negotiation. He assumed that because he had given advance warning of his visit, we had loaded all the prices and that it was therefore reasonable for him to aim at buying each book for half the marked price.

So, with a great show of flashing white teeth and joyous laughter he would suggest some outrageous figure and I would pretend to faint with shock. As I mentioned earlier about bargaining in general, unless you had a clear figure in mind as your minimum price, you had very little chance against the typhoon of a good Italian dealer. Each breath either of you took would seem to be a signal for a "really very best price, special extra discount for such large quantity, yes?"

After the Italian typhoon had swept through the front door, I would always have to say, "Please forgive me, but the fact that you are buying a lot of books is not justification for me to sell them to you at less than I paid for them. My final price is . . . "

And that would be that - until the next time the Italians came to town!

******

English dealers who come into the shop are generally looking for books I have under-priced (the price suggesting I'd bought the book more cheaply than it should have gone for) or for something impossible like the missing volume of a set. Foreign dealers, however, are much more likely to be specialists looking for books on specific subjects, or written by specific authors, and may be very pleased indeed if they can find titles in their field that I have not priced beyond their budgets. Such dealers tend also to be of the, 'Have you any more signed Mark Twains?' persuasion; that is, assuming that because you once had something unlikely that suited them, you will do so again, and again, and again . . .

Mr. and Mrs. Carter, a Canadian couple, were excellent examples. They came in one afternoon and asked if I had anything unusual by Conan Doyle. I swung round on my swivel chair and extracted from a row of books behind me a little duodecimo first edition of *The Parasite*. To a specialist dealer it must have seemed absurdly cheap, and I enjoyed the way Mr. Carter, trained dealer that he was, betrayed no emotion at all when he took the book from me - or when he bought it for what he clearly considered a bargain price. The next time the Carters appeared, I was able to bring out a nice bright copy of *Strand Magazine*, recently bought at auction, which contained the entire first edition of *The Adventures of Sherlock Holmes*. From then on, the Carters came regularly, always with the cheerfully restrained eagerness of two retrievers seeing a gun in its master's hands. Sometimes, of course, I had nothing for them, but true to their calling, they searched the shop from top to bottom anyway, hoping there was something I'd overlooked. I liked the Carters for their enthusiasm, and would always keep an eye open at auctions and fairs for anything they might want. Doing so, and showing it to them the next time they came in, gave me almost as much pleasure as I knew it gave them. My only regret was that their passion was for Conan Doyle, not someone vastly more obscure and expensive.

Other buyers who came in were less interested in the contents of books than in their appearance. These were interior decorators whose job it was to provide attractive backgrounds for wealthy people who didn't read but who knew, or had been told, that books do furnish a room - and make the room's owner look rather grand and intelligent. The decorators actually did believe that you *can* judge a book by its cover if the cover looks elegant enough, but were often disappointed to discover that the books they'd carefully selected for their height and spine turned out to be valuable for their contents as well, and hence ruinous to their decorating budgets. One such customer came twice to the shop and ahead of his third visit sent this most beguiling letter:

> Please select eight yards of leather-bound books whose spines are excellent but whose boards may be very scuffed (I care not) and are more or less the same height (octavo). Price them, knock off the usual discount, go through the usual negotiation and for once assume that I win.

Then round down to the nearest hundred and I will look in next week to give you the money and shipping instructions.

Your pauper friend,
Mark Smithson

It may sound easy, O you who lie on your chaise longue in your libraries or offices surrounded by rows of fine books, but laying hands at short notice on 24 feet of not terribly valuable books that look splendid is not an easy task for a modest provincial bookseller (I denigrate here for effect, of course), nor 24 feet of very valuable books, for that matter. For the last three feet, I had to visit our two neighbouring bookshops who were very helpful but surprised to see me, sweat on my brow and tape measure in hand, pulling down uninteresting books and piling them on their desk. Between us, we just made the last yard, on which I made no profit other than enhancing the reputation of Bankes Books in the eyes of a bookseller I had only met twice before.

Nor did decorating by the yard always achieve the desired result. Mrs. Yardley appeared in the shop one morning, told me she'd walked from the Royal Crescent – close enough for a pleasant October stroll, but today, sadly, far enough to get thoroughly soaked in an October thunderstorm. She said good morning and then went straight to the fine leather bindings, opened her handbag, and took out a carpenter's roll-up steel tape measure.

"You see," she said, "it's a birthday present for my husband and his study has got a gap of 2 feet 11 inches. In one bookcase, not the wall. And I thought it would be nice to fill the gap. With books, you see."

She asked me to hold the tape measure then, which I did with pleasure. "These nice books make 2 feet 10 inches. Now, have you got a one-inch book that would look right with these?"

£270 less discount made £240 more or less and Mrs. Yardley left looking terribly happy with a fat green carrier bag in each hand. Another satisfied customer . . .

Or so I thought!

Three days later, and a year older, Mr. Yardley came into the shop with a fat green carrier bag in each hand.

"I wonder," he said, "if you have about 3 feet of Tom Clancy books? I need to make an exchange."

Still, it's the thought that counts, isn't it?

******

Another kind of dealer, several of whom might appear almost daily in any bookshop, is the runner – a man or woman, described earlier, who runs from dealer to dealer offering a book, but who is known more familiarly in the antiquarian book business as 'a source'. Such people are very often seen at the front of a queue to get into a village fête, so that they can be first to study the charity book stall. They will feel rightly miffed if they find some amateur punter already lodged in the pole position, and will often employ some subterfuge to get in first past the silver-haired guardian of the gate - assume a worried look, say, and hurry past her, muttering, "Urgent message from hospital for Mr. Mumble."

All of this in pursuit of The Runner's Dream, which occasionally does come true (else what's a dream for?) It is that the fair's organiser, realising at the last minute that he/she has neglected to donate something to the White Elephant stall, will seize an armful of books at random from his/her own bookshelves, and dash to deliver them to the steering committee. These books will include (and this is the crux of the dream) a pristine first edition of *Casino Royale*, which will of course end up on the charity book stall priced at 50p. And to make his dream come true all the runner has to do is get to it ahead of that damned amateur . . . !

Most runners are by nature itinerant and prefer the freedom of going from place to place as they wish rather than being bound by the disciplined, daily routine of keeping a shop - and worse, having to observe following the niceties of protocol associated with that profession.

Shop Etiquette

An American entering a shop he has not visited before, feels more comfortable if the shopkeeper makes an obvious effort to be friendly as well as making it clear that he would like to sell something. Almost certainly the question, "How can I help you?" will figure quite quickly in the conversation between them. Europeans, however, tend to shrink from quick intimacies, and the English seem particularly suspicious of any attempt at even polite conversation. "How can I help you?" is regarded among the English as a sure precursor of that most embarrassing of all interchanges, The Hard Sell - and will invariably be met with, "No thanks, I'm just browsing."

Which, in turn, is a sure precursor to an early getaway, with no book purchased. I found it best, sitting as I did just across from the door, to greet all visitors with a cheerful but not effusive "Good morning." This would establish the fact that I had seen them come in so that if they wished to ask a question they would feel comfortable doing so, but would not in any sense sound threatening, or - Heaven forbid - suggest that I wanted to chat. Thereafter, visitors were left to their own devices, and if they didn't want to talk, no one was going to make them do so. A local millionaire once asked me, whilst we were talking about books, "Why do I feel safe here?"

"Because no one is trying to sell you anything," I replied, as he added another book to the pile of those I was trying to sell him.

Silence is Golden is a good general rule in a bookshop, just as it is in a library. Or in life. And when shop silence is broken, it is well to remember that anyone standing at the shelves, intently scrutinising a book, is also intently listening. One wet Saturday morning, when several people had come in to the shop to shelter as well as to look at books, Frank Bazeley who lived just up the road in Catherine Place, came in with a folio book well wrapped up in brown paper. I liked Frank. He lived with his friend Johnnie who had been a concert pianist working for most of his life playing in the orchestras of music halls. Frank, tall and handsome though bald now, had kept a pub at the Angel, Islington, and had many good stories about the people who frequented it – not a few of them ending with his having to throw someone out. He and Johnnie were, he told me, very much in love and did so wish they had met fifty years earlier.

He had been in the shop quite often and had bought several not very exciting books, so I didn't expect the one he wanted to show me now would be anything special. As he unwrapped it, being very careful not to get the desk wet, he told me that he had rescued this book from a bonfire some twenty years before. I was not encouraged by this news, but my spirits rose when Frank revealed the cover of a book I had often read about, but never seen. It was *Le Bouquet*, consisting of a collection of pictures of very beautiful hand-coloured flowers.

"Absolutely splendid," I said quietly - and knew without looking that every ear in the shop had just pricked up. I was still leery about the provenance - 'Rescued by Frank out of Bonfire'. But the book, when fully unwrapped, did not smell (the usual inheritance of a fire-damaged volume) and there seemed to have been no damage to any of the plates. I asked Frank one or two questions about it and then offered him £1000. There was an instant susurration of indrawn breath all around the room.

"Cash?" Frank asked, unable to resist playing to the gallery. "Why not?" I said, joining in - and the susurration this time was worthy of a boiling tea kettle.

Sadly, Johnnie died the following year. At the funeral, which Maryanne and I both attended, Frank told me they'd both known it was coming, but said how pleased he was, thanks to my buying that book, that they'd spent the £1000 on "a jolly good blow-out" at a seaside hotel.

*****

I am often asked by younger, less experienced bookdealers: 'What do you do, Mr. Bankes, if a customer returns with a book they recently bought from you and asks for his/her money back?'

The procedure is always the same, I explain, and must be followed in the best of friendly good humour:

1. Decide if you are willing to have the book back. (If it is one you know will sell again fairly quickly, fine; if it is not, proceed to the next step.)

2. Feigning forgetfulness, ask the customer exactly how much he/she paid you for the book, then determine why he/she wants to return it. (If he/she paid, for example £1000, then the answer will almost invariably be that he/she found the same book in another shop for less money. Most customers will admit to this.)

3. Determine the comparative conditions of your book and the newly found cheaper book, then politely ask to know the difference in price. When you have learned this - let us say it is, £300 - and assuming you do not want your book back; (at £1000 it may be one that has stood sleeping on your shelves for years, wasting space, demanding week after week of tedious dusting, and reminding you each day of your ignorant enthusiasm at that auction back in 19__, whatever-it-was) proceed immediately to the next step.

4. Dazzle the helpless customer with arithmetic. As follows: (pleasantly) - "I'm afraid Bankes Books is not a lending library. The day after you bought this book, another customer might well have bought it at the same £1250 and been happy forever after. Now I believe I explained that I pay half what I expect to sell any book for. And indeed I did pay £625 at auction for this book. I gave you a discount of £250 when you bought it. So you bought a book for £1000 which, in effect, has cost me £875 to obtain. If I take it back now I can't ethically offer it again for more than £1250. Which means the most I can give you for it is £625 - and that is assuming not just a quick sale but that the book is still in the same Fine condition it was when I sold it to you. You will therefore be out-of pocket £325. Add that to the £700 the other dealer wants, and the total will be £1275 paid for a book you already own for which you only paid £1000."

At which point the customer will usually say, 'Oh, well, I do see your point . . . ' and leave feeling he's actually made a profit of sorts.

******

And finally, shop etiquette will also involve patience while a customer's umbrella is allowed to drip onto the bookseller's desk; even more patience if the customer, with a merry laugh, spins his wet umbrella before closing it. The bookseller's patience may be even more sorely tried when a customer announces that he/she 'just loves books', and then pulls one violently from its shelf with a one-fingered heave at the top of the spine. Shop etiquette, alas, does not extend to giving lessons in the proper handling of books. But some brief comments on the subject may be of interest here.

Examining and Handling

People are often surprised by the care with which an experienced dealer will handle a book when examining it. He will get it down from a shelf, not by hooking a forefinger into the top of the spine and yanking, as just described, but by sliding a finger along the top edge and then carefully levering it downward until he can move his free hand under the lower board, with the upper board facing him. This takes some skill. If books have been packed on the shelf too tightly customers should ask the shop owner to take the book down for them. Many heads of spines have been sadly split by untutored treatment like that just described, and there is nothing the shop owner can do about it except pay a binder for the necessary repairs later.

Once the book has been safely removed from its shelf, the dealer will first examine its lower edge. What he's looking for - and hopes he doesn't find - is a felt pen slash signifying that the book is in some way faulty. Next, he will look to see if there is any triangulation: With the spine as the base and the two boards as the long legs of a theoretical triangle, he will press the boards closed to see if there is any indication of missing pages, which will almost always be plates. If the front edges of the two boards, when pressed together, can be seen to form the beginning of a triangular shape, the dealer will then place the book on an available flat surface and begin the task of collation. Properly speaking, this will involve comparing the contents of the book with a detailed list of what the contents should be, including front free fly leaves, acknowledgements pages, dedication page, etc. Nowadays the term collation is more likely to mean merely checking that the plates are 'as called for' in the instructions to the binder or in the contents listing. But before a book can be described as 'collated' a dealer must turn over every page to make sure none is torn or scribbled on.

No assumption should be made about either of these.

Dr. Johnson's *Dictionary* has been known to provide much attraction to the childish bearer of a red crayon, providing an embellishment which would not have pleased the great Doctor.

Wants

"I can't remember the exact title, but it was green and sort of this shape." (Customer draws a rectangle in the air.)

"Author?"

"Sorry, can't remember that either. But it's a lovely book. I used to have it when I was about sixteen. I'd so like my daughter to read it."

This is by no means an unusual request. And what's more, the importunate customer will be seriously miffed if he/she doesn't see you enter it immediately in that bright red spiral notebook on the side of your desk labelled 'WANTS – URGENT'. (This rubric, incidentally, is perfectly accurate – to the customer who wants frantically to find Aunt Bernice a copy of some Barbara Cartland fluff for her birthday next week, all requests are urgent. Nor will he not put much faith in your talents as a bookseller if that notebook is labelled WANTS - LATER or WANTS – DON'T BOTHER). The fact is that while some dealers do energetically pursue their customers' Wants – by advertising, telephoning other booksellers, searching through shelves at house calls – this is hard, notoriously unrewarding work, and in most cases not undertaken for any other than their oldest and most loyal customers. Nevertheless, shop etiquette demands that all Wants are duly logged in the Wants book, and moreover, that the bookseller promises to put his best ten men on to tracking it down. He will probably never hear of the book again, of course - until the customer reappears months later, asks if whatever it was has turned up, and is then baffled to see the bookseller duly entering it in his WANTS book again. But the bookseller must never give up and must always show willing, however pointless he knows the search to be; the customer may buy something one day if his name is entered in the book of WANTS. But if it is not, he will never be seen again.

Some WANTS – URGENT requests do merit their name,

however. One Saturday afternoon a very pretty blonde woman hurried to the desk and asked me, somewhat accusingly, "Have you seen my husband?" The shop was busy that day, and I'd no idea who she or her husband were, but it would have been churlish to say so - so instead I murmured that perhaps he was downstairs in the £2 room. He wasn't.

When, after quite a long time, she came back upstairs looking not at all happy, I thought of suggesting as light relief that I enter her husband's name in the WANTS-URGENT book, and see what I could do. She left before I could make the suggestion, which was probably a good thing.

It only occurred to me hours later that there might be a book entitled *My Husband* that I'd never heard of before. But by then, of course, it was too late.

The two most difficult wants to satisfy are children's books and missing volumes of sets. As with the man looking for the 'green book shaped like this', it is often the case with children's books that they go into the WANTS book with no title, no author, about this size, it's a lovely book, I want a copy for my niece, it's her birthday next week, so do you think you could get me one for Monday? The proper answer is, "No," but I, like most booksellers, am always optimistic, and would much rather say, "I'll do my very best."

A missing volume from a set is often easier to find, since one knows the set's title and author in advance. What is difficult, though, is finding a missing volume that matches its companions in appearance. I have never forgotten the conversation that followed my fleeting sense of achievement when, after several month's searching, I was finally able to hand the fugitive volume to the serious collector who had been seeking it.

"Ta Da!" I cried triumphantly, as I passed it across my desk.

"Oh," came the dismayed reply.

"Is there something wrong?"

"It's the wrong colour. It won't match the others on the bookshelf."

"It's only that the spine has faded a bit."

"But there are fourteen other volumes in the set. How am I to get them all the same colour?"

"Leave them out in the sun for five or six years?"

At least he had the kindness to offer a small smile in response.

When, after a year-long search, a bookseller at last finds a wanted book for an old customer and is then told: "Oh, I'm so sorry, I've already found it! I should have told you." No look of disappointment must cross his brow, no frown, no deep sigh. He must smile (as bravely as he can manage) and tell himself that next time it will be different.

And indeed, occasionally, he will be right.

Finds

It is astonishing how often people tuck letters, envelopes and shopping lists into books. Perhaps more surprising is the length of time such papers can stay there undisturbed; proof that the book, no matter how many times it has been sold or auctioned, has never been collated.

Surprisingly, my greatest find came from the Wednesday Market and not the shop. A regular visitor to my stall was a comfortable-looking vicar called Burgess. He was always selling, never buying, and he provided me with a regular stream of good, saleable books (all offered to me at reasonable, but not cheap prices). So consistent was his pricing, in fact, that I finally realised he must be looking up all the books he brought me in the catalogues and then setting his prices just a little below the most recent auction prices they'd fetched. Which was most sensible, but which also made me wonder, with a prickling of hairs at the back of my neck, whether the books he brought me might not have come from the shelves of his innocent and trusting flock. An unworthy thought, I decided, and one I put aside almost as immediately as I had it.

Then one Wednesday in September, I bought a nice copy of a single volume of the quarto edition (first) of Gibbon's *Decline and Fall of the Roman Empire*. I hoped that on succeeding Wednesdays Burgess might produce other volumes of the set. But he did not, somewhat to my surprise. Then one evening, about half way through collating the lone Gibbon volume, I came upon an envelope, a single quarto sheet with an address on the front. There was no postage stamp, but on closer inspection I saw an official looking rubber stamp, with a date that began 16 - -, with the last two numbers smudged. I felt this envelope must be of some value and began the process of showing it to potential purchasers. The first offer I had was £5, the next £2000. I was seriously tempted by that, but decided to put it into auction before accepting and see what happened. In the first two sales, bidding failed to reach my reserve of £2000. Then the glory day arrived; in the next auction it sold for £6000.

Out of kindness, I decided not to tell the vicar about my find. I also decided that I'd learned two most important lessons from my chance discovery: Always collate thoroughly - and never accept the first offer.

One afternoon my telephone rang and I was asked if I would like to cast my eye over the effects of a priest who had died in a hospice near Bath. I arrived that evening a little irritated because a misdirection, as I saw it, had led me past the hospice to a village some four miles away. When I came to St. Mark's, I was led down a dark corridor to Father David's room, and was told cheerfully that I had been recommended by another bookseller who had spoken most highly of me.

As I looked at the almost empty bookshelf, I could hear the hollow laughter of this jubilant bookseller, who had no doubt been delighted with the books he had found. However, on the bottom bookshelf, tucked behind an empty carton, I found a bundle of letters, the correspondence of a lonely man, now deceased: repeat prescriptions for medication, letters from St. Mark's about the conditions of his entry, two letters from the coroner's office in Bath. I looked again. The coroner? Wasn't that a bit premature? I read the coroner's letters, both of which I discovered related to the finding of a Saxon ring in what was declared to be treasure trove. But the treasure was now lost again, the second letter said. Lost? Saxon ring? Was this whole visit to be a waste of time? I looked at the three remaining books in the shelves - all sermons. Very little demand for these, I thought. Next to them was a little pile of bits and pieces: a row of First World War medals, a few more letters tied together with a pink ribbon, and a small slab of wood about 2x4 inches by half an inch deep. The medals were the usual campaign medals, but I took everything on the shelf, agreed to a small sum with the hospice administrator, wrote out two copies of a receipt and handed over one of them with my cheque.

At home, I glanced through the sermons – hardly worth the trouble of feeding and polishing the calf covers. The medals, as I knew, were not rare gallantry medals, perhaps worth a few pounds, but no great find. The little slab of wood was grimy, had some little flowers painted on what I took to be the top, and again appeared to be nothing. Except that it seemed to be too heavy for an ordinary piece of wood 2x4 inches in size. I took it to a better light, looked more closely, and finally saw a line just below the top, going round three sides of the rectangle. A pencil box for very short pencils? I wondered. I pushed on the top with my thumb, the way one tries a Chinese puzzle, and the top opened. Inside, I saw something about the circumference of an old penny, but thicker, wrapped in a piece of linen.

A moment later, there in the palm of my hand, lay a ring. A Celtic gold ring, gleaming dully. Could it be mine? I returned to the coroner's letters, which included Father David's certified statement that his own father had found the ring in a field, that the ring had been declared legally his according to the ancient laws of treasure trove, and that when his father died the ring had been left to him, date such and such. The nurse at St. Mark's had told me that in his last illness, Father David had asked a solicitor to draw up his will, leaving all his effects to the hospice. Which meant I had just bought that ring from Father David's heirs, for about £50.

I had the ring valued three times and as all valuations were much the same, I sold it to the highest offer. I then went back to the hospice, told them the whole story, and gave them half of the ring's sale price. The hospice was delighted by this wholly unexpected posthumous gift from Father David. They had already received a not inconsiderable sum under the terms of his will. Apart from the ring itself, they had given me a very exciting evening - and an especially pleasing one because I had been recommended by a bookseller who thought he had pulled a mischievous little joke on me.

******

Marjorie, tall, fair-haired, slim and neatly dressed in dark blue, came into the shop and asked me to look at her father's volumes, several of which had come from Bankes Books. Her father, who had often come into the shop when we first opened, had been a very clever man who had served for many years in Africa, and who in later years enjoyed the challenge of building himself a small, very personal library. When I went to the house, I could see that while there were some very select books, like a fine clean copy of the five volumes of *Bruce's Travels*, there were very many others that, while good books, were not in good condition and were in fact very much like what they appeared to be – interesting books bought by a man who did not like to waste money on books in good condition when good enough would do.

Marjorie explained that her mother did not wish to part with her husband's books – they had been so much a part of their life – but that there was something else she would like my advice on. She went to a desk then and took out a small leather-bound autograph book.

"I don't think there's anything else interesting in Dad's desk," she said, "but do you think this might be real?"

Only one page in the book had been used; the name, written in ink across the whole of that page was David Livingstone. On the back of the same page, written in the same hand, was: "I do not often write my autograph, but such a charming request is irresistible, and accordingly I have done so on the other side."

I looked at it for perhaps ten seconds, and told Marjorie that I had no hesitation in confirming the autograph as genuine. Once again, as with her father's books, Marjorie felt that her mother would not want the autograph book to be sold. And I have never seen it anywhere since.

Such finds as these are very rare, and provide a kind of zing of excitement to days that tend otherwise to follow an endlessly repeated routine of open the shop, sell some books, have lunch, sell some more books, close the shop, go to auctions and house sales, buy books, prepare them for sale, open the shop next morning.

Until one day, quite unexpectedly, things change . . .

"She was leaning."

But first, some illuminating afterthoughts about the odd lessons I learnt as a shopkeeper during the 20 years I sat behind the big desk at Bankes Books.

Books in the Window

Margarets Buildings enjoyed what advertising people describe as 'a high footfall' - fancy marketing language for 'Lots of people walking by all day.' We decided, therefore, that if we made the window attractive enough, there would be no need for paid advertising. This proved to be true, and as I've said earlier, the only advertising we ever did after opening was to put a notice in the local paper whenever we needed a shop assistant. (I had been told that some shops also hired models to attract custom by standing like mannequins in their windows, but my suggestion to Maryanne that we try this clever ruse, alas, did not meet with favour.)

Publishers give much thought to the kind of high-visibility

wrappers that will catch the eye on shelves, and early on we began displaying such books in the window to do just that for Bankes Books; not bodice-rippers, of course - we were above that sort of thing - but crash-bang James Bond covers, or colourful Cape and Sword wrappers proved to be just as effective. Later, we came to realise that almost any book cover featuring type large enough for people to read on the hoof, would draw attention to the rest of the books in the window. At which point we withdrew a bit from the merely blatant eye-catching approach, and became rather wittier, more subtle, and in the end, more successful at enticing customers with our window displays. The only drawback to this strategy was having to clamber into the window space to retrieve the lead book if some passer-by decided he wanted to buy it. Still, the book had done its work in the window, so I learned - or at least accepted - that if the book sold, there were no grounds for complaint about strained backs and bruised knees.

One Monday morning I put together a window display of all sorts of books about Bath, which featured, because of its eye-catching cover, a children's story called *Mr. Zinzan Comes to Bath*. The book itself seemed fairly unreadable, but I liked the title and its huge letters were visible from half way down Margarets Buildings. Just before noon, a burly New Zealander came in, bought the book without any apparent curiosity as to its contents, gave me his address in New Zealand, and asked me to send him any more Mr. Zinzan books that came my way. I'd no idea why, until Nicholas told me a week or so later that Zinzan Brooke was a super-galacto of the New Zealand All-Black rugby team, as famous down under as David Beckham was here above, and over the next three years I posted off fifteen copies of Mr. Zinzan. Then a rather plaintive letter arrived from my New Zealand friend, which stated that his (unpronounceable) town's library/zoo, or zoo/library, now boasted the largest stock of Zinzan books in the Antipodes, assured me that Bankes Books was now known among all of his friends as the finest bookshop in the Northern Hemisphere, and then asked, with grateful regret, ('sheepishly', I suppose, is more apposite for a New Zealander) if I could see my way clear to not sending any more Zinzan books to him. I wrote back at once to thank him for his generous custom and kind words, and to assure him that no more Zinzan books would ever again be dispatched to his faraway corner of the world. (A relief, actually, since Zinzan books combined those two most despised descriptives known to bookdealers: 'impossible to find' and 'worth nothing'.)

Another of our window displays - which led to fifteen fewer sales than the Zinzan books, but provoked a good deal of sniggering and giggling, consisted of the three titles: *Scouting for Boys*, *A Gay Adventurer*, and *Sixty Years a Queen*. I arranged these apparently randomly - close-ish to one another but not in an orderly line, so that people who spotted the joke could point out the potential contiguity to their less observant friends, and so think themselves pretty discerning and witty fellows.

Drawn initially by another of our window displays (I never knew which), Mr. Purvis came in regularly for several months and always went straight downstairs without speaking. I did not learn his name for some time, but on his return journey up the stairs, his thick spectacles always seemed a little misted - which didn't explain anything, but certainly got one wondering. Then one afternoon he ascended from the depths, triumphantly waving a book he had found in the £2 room - *Days of Sunshine*, was its title, its author one Laura Purvis. He took out his cheque book. "Is it all right to pay by cheque? I know a cheque for £2 can't be really popular . . . " he paused, looked around him, and pointed finally at a beautifully bound copy of *A Shropshire Lad*.

"Perhaps I could have that as well. That makes £27. . . No, I shouldn't think of making it a bit less. I'm just so delighted to have found my aunt's book. She will be overjoyed. Thank you so much."

And I never saw him again. But it was most graceful of him to buy the *Shropshire Lad*, which I don't think he wanted, just to make up for the trouble of a £2 cheque. (But, also, I suspect, he wanted to be able to say to his aunt that he'd given £27 for her book which, in my innocence, I had unwittingly consigned to the £2 room).

We tried to change the window display once a week, always with the intention of displaying well-presented, interesting books. It was too much to hope that we could always arrange things to make some sort of silly joke, but if one occurred, so much the better. One customer, I recall, said gratefully, "On my way to the station every

Monday morning I always make a detour down Margarets Buildings
to look at your window - and there is nearly always something to
make me smile, even on a wet winter morning. Thank you so much."

******

Keeping the window glass clean and its surrounding woodwork
smartly painted was no less important than the display itself. And as
I learned at the Wednesday Market, it remained excellent practice
to go outside once a week or so, walk to one end of the street or the
other, then turn around and approach the shop pretending to be just
another example of High Footfall - or, if one were in more triumphal
mood, a judge in the Best Bookshop in the Country competition.

Cleaning may also cover the cleaning of books themselves. I
learned early on that passers-by would always stop to look in the window if I were displaying a set of handsomely bound, well-polished
books with their titles on the spine clearly legible - but not, I also
learned, shining as if newly re-gilded. Shining book titles, known as
gleamers in the trade, are curiously unattractive to English customers - although to American eyes it seems to be a case of "the more
gleaming, the better".

(In a bookshop, cleaning may mean more than cleaning the spine.
Victorian books often suffer from foxing, sometimes caused by damp,
but more often because using pulped wood instead of rag when making the white paper for pages in the nineteenth century, offered a
considerable economy - and a critical one where large print runs were
required. Unfortunately, it also meant that a chemical reaction in the
paper produced small brown marks - like the brown spots on ageing
pears. This effect was particularly evident on engraved plates, very
often because of the different quality of paper used for them; some
badly foxed plates can appear to be almost entirely blackened. When
cleaning such damaged books for resale, it is not uncommon for pages and plates to be washed in a light bleach - which does clean the
paper effectively, but as those who regularly handle Victorian books
know, makes the pages seem curiously dead to the touch. To some,
a nice clean page is preferable to a foxed or partially blackened one,

no matter what the effect upon the paper's 'feel' may be. It should be pointed out to customers, though, by any dealer selling a 'washed' book, that if the bleach has been used too liberally, there is a chance the paper may actually disintegrate after a few years. I tend to believe that this caveat is almost never raised when doing business in rare and antiquarian bookshops.)

When choosing books for window displays, the shopkeeper must always keep in mind that bright sunshine can cause boards to curl and their covers to fade - both of which sorts of damage is irreparable. It is prudent, therefore, not to display very valuable books in windows that take direct sunlight. Direct sunlight is an enemy of books - but an enemy luckily not too often met with in the U.K.

The Back Room

If the window display may be likened to a beckoning finger promising pleasures within, then the 'Back Room' may fairly be described as The Hall of Hidden Delights.

The Back Room of an ordinary retail bookshop is popularly supposed to be inhabited by furtive men in long mackintoshes asking for their purchases to be wrapped, please, in plain brown paper. Not so with Antiquarian and Rare bookshops, however. Their Back Rooms are used to store books destined specially for the eyes of visiting dealers, or as a space for keeping incomplete sets, or as a hospital for books with, for example, missing plates that must be restored before the book can be sold, or damaged bindings that must be made perfect again.

Veteran booksellers, who like nothing better than showing off to the young, will happily describe to wide-eyed novices the famed Back Rooms of old, where long wooden benches covered with ancient newspapers, pots of glue and arcane stitching tools, were overseen by grizzled booksellers with pebble-lensed spectacles on their noses, clandestinely manufacturing fine first editions from the tattered scraps of a hundred ruined books piled in a shadowy corner by the stove. That practice has long since disappeared - but the tradition remains (along with the romance) and each visiting dealer is convinced in his heart of hearts that one day *this* bookshop will harbour a proper, old-fashioned Back Room of Treasures. And if he has been sensible enough to let the shopkeeper know well in advance what sort of treasure he is seeking, there is some small chance that the very book he seeks will actually be produced for him.

******

As a resting place for incomplete sets of books, the Back Room of an antiquarian book shop fulfils a function roughly equivalent to that of a scrap yard: That is, the only place you find a hub cap for a 1957 Jowett Javelin, or volume 12 of OUP's 1912 deluxe edition of the complete works of Thackeray. Obviously, if the missing volume or volumes can be found this way, the full set can be restored for much less than the cost of buying the whole collection anew. And if the Back Room of their favourite bookseller lets them down, they can always try one of the dozens of book finding services that advertise each month in literary and specialist publications, and can also be found online. Antiquarian bookdealers, will also join in the search to help their regular customers. But nothing is as satisfying as stumbling unexpectedly on that elusive missing volume in The Back Room of a musty old second hand bookshop - or indeed a magnificent one like Bankes Books!

******

A dealer may have leapt with glee upon a book which at first sight seemed to be a valuable first edition but which more thorough collation has proved to be missing a plate, or have a torn plate, or one 'coloured by a childish hand'. Having paid a lot of money for this book, it now becomes the bookseller's dream to lay hands on another copy of the same book, in equally less than unblemished condition, but with the desired plate intact and in perfect condition. If this dream comes true, the Back Room will then become a Book Hospital, and he will go to work with his trusty scalpel (usually a sharp Stanley knife) to remove the good plate from the book he's just acquired, hopefully match its stitching holes to those made by the stitcher in the margin of the book he's repairing, (if they don't match he will have to paste rather than stitch the perfect plate into place - less than ideal, but still acceptable). And after a few minutes careful work, lo! the first book has become as described 'with plate at p.xx matched' rather than 'lacks plate at p.xx'

A less scrupulous dealer might find it convenient not to draw attention to this bit of handiwork. But I strongly advise honesty in the matter.

The Shopkeeper and the Seductress

This subject needs to be addressed to bookshop owners as a warning because unfortunately, what I'm going to describe is not uncommon, particularly where the layout of a shop incorporates an unmanned downstairs sales room, as Bankes Books does.

In conversations with a number of my fellow bookshop owners I was made to understand that dealers alone in their shops could sometimes become the targets of bored women or even schoolgirls out for a bit of excitement. I have never considered myself much of a target for anyone, bored or otherwise, but a year or so after the shop opened I began to notice that a senior girl from the one of the local Girls' Schools used to come in more frequently than seemed reasonable in search, she said, of Angela Brazil books. One day this girl came up the stairs from the £2 room rather more heavily made up than usual, and asked if I could come downstairs and help her look for a particular title. At that moment I was chatting with two old customers about a rare book they were interested in, said I couldn't come downstairs, and more or less waved the girl away. Ten minutes later we were interrupted by the girl again, this time ascending the stairs with a rolled-up piece of paper about 18 inches wide in her hand, saying that she wished me to examine it. I rather rudely continued my conversation with my customers and again waved her away. Angered by this, she flung the paper onto my desk, and stormed out of the shop in a huff. Later, after closing, I unrolled the paper she'd thrown down - and was confronted with a full-length, well, not exactly self-portrait, but a self-nude.

Luckily, the story ends there. The succession of girl 'customers' from that particular school stopped quite abruptly and I assumed that the young lady with the fanciful self-portrait told her friends that there was no naughty fun to be had at Bankes Books.

******

I am sure she will forgive me for telling this - in fact, she'll probably relish it - but I must include the glamorous Mrs. Desola as one of the serious hazards faced by the lone bookshop proprietor in Bath - and probably elsewhere. She seemed pleasant enough when she first came in looking for a birthday present for her husband. It was raining, and she was wearing a long black mackintosh over blue jeans, so I hardly recognised her when she returned a week later wearing a tight scarlet top open at the neck which left no doubt as to the generosity with which nature had endowed her. She had dark, swept-back hair, lots of eye makeup and gave me the sort of dazzling, self-confident smile I expect Hollywood starlets offer to important film producers at casting conferences. She sat down opposite me at my desk and began fluttering the pages of the present I'd found for her husband - a quite expensive early motoring book about Jaguars. I noticed (it was hard not to) that she was leaning across the desk rather further than was necessary to examine the photographs in the book, and finally realising that the undone buttons down her front had not got that way by accident, I stood up rather abruptly, quoted the book's price, wrapped it as quickly as I could and put it in one of our bags. She paid by credit card, I thanked her and said goodbye.

Rather than discourage her, however, I fear that my apparent indifference to her charms must have seemed like a challenge, because she came back again two weeks later 'To buy a golfing book for a boyfriend', she said pointedly. I selected two good books from the golf and tennis shelves (always give the customer a choice) and left them on the desk for her to look at. She told me how much she loved old books. I noted with relief that today she was wearing an un-provocative dark blue suit, and sat down across from her to explain why her friend, though loving both books, would probably prefer the one signed by Henry Cotton, even though it was the more expensive. It was at this point I had to stifle a yelp as I felt the pointed toe of her court shoe start to work its way up the inside of my left trouser leg.

As no Edwardian etiquette book I'd ever seen included advice on 'What does A do next?' in this situation, I decided to risk stiletto gash by quickly withdrawing my leg, leaping to my feet, and immediately starting a romantically neutral discussion of prices and possible discounts - only just resisting the temptation to offer 50% off 'if only you'll go away now, and not come back!'

Finally catching on, and actually shrugging her shoulders as she rose, Mrs. Desola picked up her book and walked away - wondering, I felt quite sure, who in the world she might give some ridiculous golfing book to as a present.

(It may be that readers now expect me to tell them tales of customers asking for nudge-nudge-wink-wink 'special books' in plain wrappers. Sorry, readers. That subject, like this section of my memoirs, is now closed.)

Good Moments

Sometimes in a bookshop there are illuminating moments. One summer afternoon, a number of American students, twittering like starlings, came into the shop. They were doing a summer tour of 'Yurop' following graduation from University, and everything was joyously exciting to them. They wanted to know which was the oldest book in the shop, which the most expensive, how were the books arranged, did I have a copy of *To Kill a Mockingbird* - all the usual questions young Americans ask. A tall, rather austere-looking girl wandered over to the floor-to-ceiling wall of leather-bound books and began looking at the fly leaves, book by book. This, as already described, was the classic technique of a book thief, checking the prices in order to establish which were worth stealing. Suddenly the girl let out a yelp of joy and held up a nicely bound copy of *Bleak House*, an early edition of the novel in book form. The other girls gathered round her, telling her it was a beautiful book, that it was their favourite, that she was soooo-oo lucky to have found it. I looked over, and I swear she

winked at me. "It's not that. This book belonged to my Great-Grand-
mother! I've always dreamed of finding one. See? Here's her name."
She carried the book across to the desk and read us the inscription
on the fly-leaf: "Adelaide Dickinson, Christmas 1870 from her friend,
Jane Thomas. Isn't it cool!"

Of course, despite prolonged protestations, I convinced her to
accept the book as a gift. When she finally took it - hugged it, actually
- all of her friends applauded - and then, curiously, each chose and
bought something else from the shelves 'as a memento of Bath.'

******

Early one morning in summer, I was reading at my desk when
the shop door opened and a little girl with enormous dark eyes asked
me if I had any poetry books by Rabindranath Tagore. I said we
did, indeed, and sent her downstairs where I knew there were two
Tagores, *Fireflies* and *Red Oleanders*. After quite an interval, she came
back up, beaming and carrying both books. While I took her money
and wrapped the books, she told me in impeccable, slightly accented
English, that she was from Mexico, and that the love of Tagore was
not hers but her grandmother's. She was twelve, she said, was called
Lucia, and planned to be coming to school in England soon. I was en-
chanted and asked if she would write to me when she got home and
tell me if her grandmother had liked the books. She said she would.
We exchanged several letters.

Two months later, she arrived back in Bath with her parents, and
the four of us, with Maryanne, had lunch and a pleasant afternoon in
our garden. Some weeks later I came across a signed copy of Tagore's
Crescent Moon, one of the works that earned him his Nobel Prize in
1913, and immediately sent it off to Mexico. Lucia's father explained
later that he had decided that such a special present should be kept
for Christmas. There followed a regular correspondence (by what is
so accurately called snail mail). Whenever Lucia returned to England
she always came to see us. On one such visit she expressed an interest
in making films, said that she hoped film might be her career, and
declared that she would certainly make a film about Maryanne and

me, and above all about Bankes Books. I am confident that she will do
so, and I anticipate the production of that film daily.

******

After nearly twenty years, the shop seemed well-established and
was making a living. We still went to the occasional book fair, and
had learned that the proper answer to "How's the shop?" is a cau-
tious "Not too bad" or "Mustn't grumble". We also learned to treat
every such enquiry as if it came from a rapacious landlord eager to
increase the rent. In fact our landlord did come in a few weeks before
rent review day. I did not know him - all our dealings had been done
by post - but he was a tall man of about fifty, and I saw him looking
alertly around the shop as I completed a sale to a customer. This was
in the middle of a recession (isn't it always?) and so when he told me
his name and then announced, "I'm your landlord", I was filled with
fear that, as he had just seen me make a sale he would immediately
increase the rent. I stood up. I'm six foot three but he was taller, so I
sat down again.

"I do hope you're not going to increase the rent?" I said.

"Do you think I'm mad?" he replied, with a huge grin. "You pay
regularly and you keep the place looking nice. No, I'll go back to Birmingham and leave things as they are."

To myself, I thought, *What an excellent man of business you are - and
how very English. But then Birmingham, in my view, has always been the Capital
of Common sense . . .*

And Then . . .

Seven months later, almost to the day, I was standing in the kitch-
en making a cup of coffee when my legs gave way and I found myself
lying on the floor unable to move. In due course I found myself lying
in a hospital bed recovering from a stroke, which seemed as good a
place as any to assess my new situation. So I did.

First, the lease of the shop was due for a breakpoint in four
months and Sarah, with her usual calm courage and good sense,

elected to take it on herself, and use the shop to sell the fine art prints she'd been dealing in at flower shows and antiques fairs for the past several years. She was already an experienced and highly successful print dealer, possessed of that rare eye for what's 'right', inherited from her mother, that makes all the difference in that business. And as she'd already been showing prints in one corner of Bankes Books for more than a year now, it seemed a perfect solution to the issue of the lease.

Next, having been told by my doctors that when I left hospital a month or so hence, I would have 'at best limited use of my left leg and left arm', but 'happily (sic) only slightly impaired service on the right-hand side', I had to face the fact that dealing from the shop would no longer be feasible. Hopping about on one leg, dropping the books I tried to pull from the shelves, and then not being able to pick them up again - or wrap any I'd sold, or hit the right buttons on the credit card machine, etc., etc. - simply did not match my vision of the jolly bookseller of Bath.

All was not lost, though. I reasoned that if a removals company could transport all of Bankes Books' books to a self-storage lock-up, and if I hired someone reliable to bring a boxful or two to my new, invalid-friendly flat each week (I was told I couldn't manage at Brock Street any longer, as it bristled with stroke-unfriendly stairs), I could continue dealing online and by telephone, with relatively little dif-ficulty. I still had an excellent right hand that was already versed in the skills required to use a computer. I could certainly expect to sell enough books to pay for an assistant to collect and post them, to cov-er the costs of postage and wrapping materials (brown paper, bubble wrap, packaging tape, labels and so on), plus to create and maintain a web-site at Abe-books. I already had the books to sell - and a loy-al client base created over twenty years that stretched from Bath to London, and on across the oceans to faraway lands. Even if I were utterly immobilised, I told myself, my brain still functioned like a steel trap - which meant I could still do the thing I'd learned to love doing most: Sell books.

With that settled, I felt hopeful enough to turn my attention to the third and final item on the list: Getting better. I was told that

once out of hospital and settled in my new digs, I could begin a daily
routine of physiotherapy that would slowly improve the strength and
mobility in my left arm and leg. I might even be able to walk again
fairly normally if I stuck to it, they assured me. Parallel bars played a
large role in this therapeutic regime, as did a rubber squeeze ball and
some curious apparatus that involved elasticised ropes. And I did try
my best; I promise I did - because I'd have been more than pleased
to have been able to walk fairly normally again, or even abnormally
(which I did, in fact manage, aided by a stick, for a year or so after leaving hospital). But regimes that involve physical rather than
mental activity have never been my strong suit. Nor did Maryanne's
insistence, perfectly true, that I simply wasn't trying hard enough spur
me on to greater and greater feats of recovery on the parallel bars. I
won't say I actually gave up on the exercise regime. It's more that I
became steadily more used to my condition and steadily less interested in exercising until finally, well, I did give up on it, didn't I?

I settled in my new temporary flat in Rivers Street, (just two
streets from our Brock Street flat to make it easy on Maryanne) and
found a suitable assistant and prepared to return to selling books. The
Bankes Books stock had been moved by then to a big lock-up storage
space at Pickford's Warehouse in the Lower Bristol Road. I worked
out an identification system so my assistant could find the books I
wanted brought to Rivers Street. Nicholas came in one week-end and
re-arranged the sitting room like a library, with tall shelves against
two walls, a long book table ranged along a third wall, and a desk and
three smaller tables grouped near the front window creating a kind of
ship's bridge/nerve centre where all necessary communications and
business gear could be reached by simply turning myself about in a
big swivel chair. Sarah and Maryanne kept my kitchen well stocked, I
learned how to use a tin opener and a microwave oven one-handed,
nice Mrs. Davies came in twice a week to clean the flat and change
my bedding, invalid handles were installed all over the place in de-
fence against falling - it wasn't nearly as much fun as life before the
stroke, but it worked pretty well and I saw, with relief, that I'd probably be able to carry on this way for some time.

Once the kinks were worked out, I found that my system for

finding, transporting and posting books worked smoothly enough. But because I was selling online now, and hence sight-unseen, I also found that every slight defect in a book being offered must be described accurately and not minimised. One day, while making a list of tiny fox marks in an early copy of *Tom Sawyer* that I was asking £100 for, it occurred to me that if estate agents were legally subjected to similar constraints, a great deal of wasted time, expense and temper fraying could be avoided. Because unlike houses or flats, if a book I post to an online buyer is not exactly as described, it may be returned with a request for its purchase price *plus* return postage to be paid immediately. Which is, beyond the hassle involved, rather financially counterproductive.

Bargain-hunting was no less fierce when dealing online. Many of my sales were preceded by predatory suggestions about lowering the price if payment was made directly to me, thus cutting out Abe Books' commission. I always said no to this. Abe Books' commission for advertising dealers' wares on their website is, in truth, quite high - but I could not have done business without them and the idea of short-changing them always struck me as rather churlish. Besides, I'd have had to inform them that I was withdrawing such-and-such a title from my site if I took payment for it privately - and of course they'd know why. I found packing books with one hand to be a risky business, and after several had slipped from my knees and crashed to the floor, invariably damaging a board or the spine (which, of course, required further confession on my website), I decided to hire Luke as my Postal Executive. With a sunny smile, he would arrive each Tuesday morning and collect a modest pile of books destined to be packaged, addressed and sent on their way to various parts of the world. With the exception of one book which went to Canterbury via Western Australia, all the books Luke dispatched went smoothly from Bath to their destinations. Sometimes flurries of emails about apparent delays would appear, but the books always turned up in the end, and I found, with some satisfaction, that I had successfully married my early life in the computer industry to the more ancient one of book selling.

One day I received a PayPal money order from America in payment for a Roycrofter edition of Walt Whitman's *Song of Myself*. Unfortunately, the book had just been sold, and full of apologies, I sent an email offering a full refund. The customer, Sandy Barton of Buffalo, New York, responded by return email. I replied to her response, and soon the ether was thick with our correspondence. During the next two years an exchange of well over a thousand emails took place with this charming Buffalonian (soon known to my grand-daughter Evelyn as Lady Buffalo). Although our emails ran rather longer than the letters in *84 Charing Cross Road*, we both agreed that the interchange between Bath and Buffalo, plus the eventual meeting of the protagonists, might make delightful reading. With insouciant enthusiasm, Sandy made plans to come to Bath to finally meet 'The Man She'd Met on the Internet'. Since that meeting she has 'collated' our emails, typed them out as a final manuscript (preceded by 13 revisions) and has now published it online at Amazon. She will be happy to sell you, dear reader, a copy of *Abjectedly Yours* - or several. Thank you.

******

I can't remember what administrative error of mine drew Michael Smith from Austin, Texas to my room. I mentioned laughingly that the only person from Austin I knew was a man called Al Dale who had spent some time with me in Bratislava working for the UN, and I supposed Mr. Smith knew him? Much to my surprise Michael replied that his best friend's sister was Al's widow, and that he had died a year or two previously suffering from Alzheimer's. This coincidence set us off well and I soon realised that Michael was not only much cleverer than I, but had a much better organised memory. He was generally a very exceptional person.

When he was working his way through college, he told me, he saw an old ramshackle house and bought it for practically nothing. Then he in effect re-built it, re-wired it, put in new plumbing, painted it, and in doing so equipped himself with the knowledge and skill for each trade involved. He then sold the brightly shining new house and with the proceeds bought another near ruin and refurbished it. He now has a string of houses he rents out, looking after any little problems they may develop himself. Inevitably, Michael has the self-confidence of a man who has successfully made his own living. He wears this confidence quietly and with dignity, and his coruscating intelligence makes any conversation a great pleasure.

I count myself lucky that, in coming to visit his daughter at the Sorbonne, Michael took the time to stop off at Bath. His Paris sojourns became regular – every four months or so – and always included a few days stopover in Bath. He said he always looked forward with anticipation to my 'Texas Box' filled with books I had put aside for him; that, along with some much needed good conversation. He has bought a considerable number of very nice books from me and in doing so, has greatly swelled the Law School Fund for my grandson Charles William. A good result all round.

******

As the weeks passed, it was not unpleasant to be told by Sarah that she was often stopped in the street and asked about her father, with gratifying remarks about how much his bookselling skills were missed -   almost always by people whose book buying skills I much missed myself.

Next month, I shall be eighty. A landmark that once meant an old man had spent an entire decade clinging on with his fingertips past the allotted three score years and ten; an accomplishment once celebrated by a host of awestruck relations and friends who would gather round him, raise their glasses in heartfelt toast, and then settle down to telling each other stories about how long ago it was since they'd last met. Nowadays, eighty is nothing more than a pause to draw breath in the Race to the Century. Nowadays, eighty years is celebrated by a round of golf with his octogenarian mates, at which our hero means to score less than his age in a round as good as any he has played all week.

I am confined to bed now - no longer in my Rivers Street flat, but in a splendid nursing home called Bridgemead, with a caring staff and a window over-looking the river Avon. I am also embarked on a third career, selling books from a prone position (yes, still selling!). Though literally single-handed, I am able still to show that a third career can be profitable. Also, though seriously one-sided now, I can still flutter a handful of puns at a moment's notice. More importantly, I can fling a book onto my iPad® or Kindle® - and using only two arthritic fingers and a brilliantly gifted thumb, I can magnify the text so that failing eyes can still read my favourite books and venture on new ones.

I think I started this book with the bold statement that I did not set out to be an antiquarian bookdealer, and I hope we have seen that I found myself as a proud member of what Napoleon called 'a nation of shopkeepers'.

And somewhere I warned that dealers should not be collectors. I can modify this by saying that while I no longer collected books because they were friends, I certainly collected friends because of books. An army of really valuable friends, one regiment led by Sandy with her redoubtable courage, and another by Michael with his diamond-sharp intelligence. I am very lucky, and can say with gratitude, that books *do* furnish the mind.

******

VOCABULARY

Antiquarian
In the antique trade, this word is generally used to describe an object over 100 years old. An antiquarian book is probably early Victorian or older. There is no hard and fast rule.

Blackening
Severe browning almost blacked out a plate and caused the bookseller to resort to washing (q.v.) the offending plate.

Block
If the boards and pastedown pages of a book were removed, the remaining text, advertisement and index pages form the block. The edges may be decorated by marbling or a fore-edge painting.

Book
When a book is laid on a table it is seen to have a lower cover (the cover on the table) and an upper cover (the cover showing when the book is closed). These are joined by the spine (often called the back). The pages of the book are called the block, and the block has a top edge, a front edge and a bottom edge. When the book is opened, the front pastedown joins the stitched block to the inside of the upper cover. The part of the pastedown page which is not pasted down is the front free flyleaf. This is sometimes followed by other blank pages, also known as free fly leaves. On the last of these is printed the title of the book – just the title, no more. This is the half-title. Next comes the title-page, bearing the title, author, place of publication, publisher and date of publication. The title-page, always on the right hand side, is on the recto. On the back of the recto is the verso page, which bears the publishing history, beginning with the month and date of this, the first edition. If this page is blank, it can be assumed there have been no previous editions. It is sometimes confusing to people when the only line on the verso says, 'First published May 1948'. This seems to imply that the copy they are holding is not a first edition. There is

no need to worry – the book is indeed a first edition. And this will be disproved only if there is a second line saying, perhaps, 'reprinted July 1948'. All reprints and new editions are listed on this page (a reprint is the book printed again with no changes. A new edition may have some or substantial changes.). Opposite the publishing history page might be page 1, or possibly the verso of a frontispiece, whose recto will face page 1. It may also be that opposite the publishing history page will be found the Dedication page, the Acknowledgements page and the Contents page. At the end of the Contents list will be a list of plates and maps. Now comes the main block of the book, each chapter beginning on a right hand page. The last page of the book, before the Index, should be at The End or End of Vol. The latter is sometimes the only indication that there are other volumes. After the last page comes the Index, followed either by the rear free flyleaves or a free pastedown page, then the rear pastedown page, pasted to the lower board.

Books were published in paper covers, the purchaser deciding on the type of binding he wanted for his new book. Very often this would be a standard binding to match other books in his library. Bookbinders were legion, and formed one of the major users of hides from the tannery. So the library might require books bound in full calf, with Cambridge panels to both boards. Full calf would be smooth leather stretched over boards, and the Cambridge panels would be a raised panel matching the shape of the book. Half calf would mean a calf spine, projecting perhaps half an inch over each board. The corners of each board would also be protected with full calf. Quarter bound describes a book with the leather spine projecting over the boards as with half bound books, but with no protective binding at the corners.

Other forms of binding are full morocco, where morocco is goat, half and quarter morocco, diced morocco, vellum, cloth, and moire cloth. These are described under their respective alphabetical place.

Book hospital
It is not unusual for booksellers to keep wounded copies of rare books

– books with pages missing, pages torn, boards faded. These books may then be used to supply books with other defects, allowing a marriage to take place where one good page from a bad book is 'married' to a book which lacks that particular page. The marriage is recorded as being without issue.

Book size

Book dealers like to demonstrate their astonishing familiarity with the world of books by sticking to the notations of the middle ages when indicating the sizes of books. These were based on the number of folds which could be made from a larger piece of paper. Thus folio, later called foolscap by stationers, made eight leaves when folded, and sixteen pages approximately thirteen inches tall by twelve inches wide. There are various large beasts such as elephant folio, but more usually folio is the largest size, with quarto (about the size of A4) the most usual size for a large book.

Quarto is pretty near A4 and the book measures 6 in. by 9 in. Then comes duodecimo, measuring 5 in. by 7 ¾in. While quarto is approximately the size of a modern novel, early to mid-nineteenth-century novels were commonly published as three-volume duodecimo sets, described as 3 vol. 12 mo.

Miniature books are those not exceeding 3 in. in height.

Break

In order to loosen the block so that plates may be easily removed, a breaker may hold one cover in one hand and the other cover in the other hand and snap the spine so that the object is achieved. This practice is greatly frowned upon unless the book is already hospital case, when it is merely a question of rescuing the wounded. Curiously one never hears of a void copy being broken.

Breaker

A book suitable for breaking.

Breaker
One who breaks a book (secretly, in the dark with vampires fluttering around).

Browning
Where brown spots or patches appear on a page, more usually on a plate of a mid–late Victorian book. Up to this time rags were used for the production of paper until it was discovered that wood seemed to make a good substitute and was considerably cheaper (to the natural rage of the rag-and-bone men). However, acid in the wood resulted in spots appearing on plates made from mashed wood. The brown spots were called 'foxing' and are attributed rightly in some cases, to dampness.

Cloth binding
Nowadays only the spine of a book is bound in cloth, the boards being covered in paper.

Colophon
The statement printed after the last page of the book showing printing details (name of type, printer, press, and number printed). Below this would be shown, in manuscript, the number of this copy, the size of the edition and the signatures of author, illustrator etc.

Commission bid
A bid left with the auctioneer. If several commission bids are left, the auctioneer will set the entry point of bidding at the lowest bid after separate commission bids have knocked each other out. For example, if three bids are left, of £20, £30 and £35, the auctioneer can start the bidding in the room at £35 as this will knock out the other two.

Damp stained
When the great enemy of all books – damp – has somehow entered the book, not necessarily through one or other of the boards. The stain will take the form of an irregular line across the page, with discolouration below the line. If there appears to be damp-staining to

one page only, there is reason to suspect that the page has been taken from another copy of the book to replace a page in an even worse condition.

De Luxe edition
Often published simultaneously with, a day or two before, or more usually never at all, a de luxe edition is printed on specially luxurious paper, signed by author and illustrator (sometimes by publisher only), bound with vellum boards, and has upper and lower boards closed with a silken tie.

Diced
A full morocco or full calf binding scratched criss-cross on both upper and lower covers.

Dog
A pejorative term for a book which looked attractive to the book dealer when he bought it, but which has remained on his shelves so long that he realises it is unsaleable at a price a little higher than he paid for it.

Drop-off number
On the verso of the title page can be found the printing history of the book, copyright ownership, typeface used and other technical printing information. Where there is a row of ten numbers, these are used to show in which issue or edition the book was published. Where all ten numbers are present, the book will be in the first issue. In the next issue the '10' is dropped off, then the '9' and so on. There is no general standard for this practice, intended for the use of publishers and booksellers only, and such arcane matters are not for the delight of the general public or dealers.

Dust wrapper
Booksellers, being superior people, glorify what ordinary people call a dust jacket by calling it a dust wrapper, abbreviated d.w. These were originally plain pieces of paper whose purpose was to protect the

book's boards (covers) in transit. Publishers, being wily folk, soon realised that, when displayed in a window or on a counter, an attractive
design was more likely to sell a book than a plain wrapper.

Fore-edge painting

If a book is held by placing the lower board on the palm of one hand
with the fingers supporting the spine, the other hand can be used to
fan the fore edge of the block. If the book with fanned fore edge is
held in a vice so that the fore edge provides a suitable surface, this
can be decorated with a view or religious scene. Such paintings were
not uncommon on prayer books, no doubt intended to amuse a child
during a long and boring sermon. An eighteenth-century fore-edge
painting can be distinguished from a modern one by the fact that,
when the book is closed, no trace of the painting is evident. A modern
painting leaves a smudge or smear when the book is closed.

Frayed

Sometimes the edges of a book's block appear to have been rubbed
harshly, giving the impression of fraying cloth.

Fugitive

Adjective applied to colours (usually green or purple) which react to
bright sunlight and fade. Sometimes when one book has been standing across another, protecting some of it from the rays, an unsightly
line on the 'protected' book can result, and the book whose covers are
evenly faded seems less undesirable, after all. Too late, alas!

Gleamer

Bookbinders left to exercise their own judgment will gild a well-bound
book with bright and shiny lettering to the spine. Such brightness can
sometimes be toned down a little if the book dealer begs that eighteenth and nineteenth-century books tend to lose their brightness in
one or two hundred years. But book buyers are strange animals and
some would prefer to buy a bright and shiny gleamer rather than a
dull, faded – dignified – book.

Graingerise

In the mid-1800s when photography was still a wonder imitating Art, it was considered something special to illustrate books with relevant photographs. For instance, George Eliot's *Romola* would have a photograph of a statue mentioned on one page stuck to a blank page, itself stuck into the block of the book. The practice was popularised by one Grainger, renowned because of these 'art' books.

Guard

See *Off-set*.

Half morocco

Books are said to be half morocco bound when the spines and corners of both upper and lower covers are bound in morocco. The covers are usually marbled.

Incunabulum

Latin for cradle and used to describe 'cradle' books, printed near the birth of printing. A pre-1500 book is often called an incunable (bad Latin to show off our poor classical education) and for the same reason we call a collection 'incunables' instead of 'incunabula'.

Limited edition

Books usually printed on private presses, for which the size of the edition was decided in advance and so stated in the colophon.

Lithography

The art of drawing (*Greek lithos*, *stone* and *grapho* (write)) on a plate suitable for printing.

Moire cloth binding

In the mid-nineteenth century publishers felt that plain cloth bindings could be made more attractive by adopting a rippled or watered effect. In textile weaving, this effect is known as moire.

Marriage
See *Hospital*.

Morocco
Before the days of paper and printing (about the last quarter of the fifteenth-century) writing was carried out on goatskin, scraped until it was almost translucent. Goatskin was also used, after being dyed in red dye, for covering the boards used as covers for books.

Muslin
Loosely woven cotton cloth.

Off-set
The ink of an engraving sometimes leaves a shadow on the facing page. This is unattractive and to some extent devalues the book. To protect against this, eighteenth and nineteenth-century plates were often given a guard sheet, a plain transparent sheet between plate and facing page.

Out of series copy
A copy of a limited edition without the required number, number printed or signatures. This may well be one of a dozen or so copies printed by the printer for his friends, a patron etc.

Quarter morocco
Books are said to be quarter morocco bound when the spines are bound in morocco with about half an inch covering marbled covers, both upper and lower covers.

Plus one
If you leave a bid with an auctioneer, say £500, it is possible that a round of bidding will end with an opposing bid of £500. The auctioneer can then bid 'plus one', and secure the lot for £550 or £500 plus whatever increment he has been adopting so far.

Porter's bid
Do not be surprised if you find yourself bidding against a porter. This will be because another dealer, unwilling to disclose his identity to the auctioneer, or feeling it necessary to be at another auction, has left a bid for the lot with one of the porters. This practice is increasingly unnecessary as dealers realise they can bid at several auctions at once on the Internet, and have to get out of bed only to pay and collect on successful bids.

Private press books
Books published in small numbers whose attraction lies in the beauty of the types selected and the way the pages are laid out. Very few of these presses operated to make a profit: their ambition was to be known for their quality.

Source
Someone who appears in a bookshop from time to time offering an attractive book. Fierce cross-questioning by the book dealer will usually reveal that the book is 'from my grandfather's collection' and this explanation will often satisfy the shopkeeper.

Toning
Where the whole of a page has turned a light brown.

Vellum
A full calf or full goatskin scraped almost to translucency, used as a medium on which to write, or as a binding. The appearance is white and marks easily.

Washing
To make pages affected by browning or severe foxing appear clean, a technique known as 'washing' was used. This involved the use of bleach and if pages were washed in a solution with too much bleach, they assumed a lifeless look, besides, appearing too clean. Sometimes this was better than the very black colour of a heavily browned page, but it could spoil a fine plate to such an effect that a 'marriage' was indicated.

Yapp
When the binding of a book overlaps the upper and lower sides of a book block by about half an inch, it is known as a yapp binding. Very often a yapp binding is made of suede.